theatre & protest

theatre & protest

Lara Shalson

palgrave

First published 2017 by
Palgrave

Palgrave in the UK is an imprint of Macmillan Publishers Limited, registered in England, company number 785998, of 4 Crinan Street, London N1 9XW.

Palgrave® and Macmillan® are registered trademarks in the United States, the United Kingdom, Europe and other countries.

ISBN 978–1–137–44309–0 paperback

This book is printed on paper suitable for recycling and made from fully managed and sustained forest sources. Logging, pulping and manufacturing processes are expected to conform to the environmental regulations of the country of origin.

A catalogue record for this book is available from the British Library.

A catalog record for this book is available from the Library of Congress.

Printed in China

contents

series editors' preface

The theatre is everywhere, from entertainment districts to the fringes, from the rituals of government to the ceremony of the courtroom, from the spectacle of the sporting arena to the theatres of war. Across these many forms stretches a theatrical continuum through which cultures both assert and question themselves. Theatre has been around for thousands of years, and the ways we study it have changed decisively. It's no longer enough to limit our attention to the canon of Western dramatic literature. Theatre has taken its place within a broad spectrum of performance, connecting it with the wider forces of ritual and revolt that thread through so many spheres of human culture. In turn, this has helped make connections across disciplines; over the past 50 years, theatre and performance have been deployed as key metaphors and practices with which to rethink gender, economics, war, language, the fine arts, culture and one's sense of self.

Theatre & is a long series of short books that hopes to capture the restless interdisciplinary energy of theatre and performance. Each book explores connections between theatre and some aspect of the wider world, asking how the theatre might illuminate the world and how the world might illuminate the theatre. Each book is written by a leading theatre scholar and represents the cutting edge of critical thinking in the discipline.

We have been mindful, however, that the philosophical and theoretical complexity of much contemporary academic writing can act as a barrier to a wider readership. A key aim for these books is that they should all be readable in one sitting by anyone with a curiosity about the subject. The books are challenging, pugnacious, visionary sometimes and, above all, clear. We hope you enjoy them.

Jen Harvie and Dan Rebellato

prologue

As this book was about to go to press, an unusual thing happened at the theatre. After the curtain call for *Hamilton: An American Musical* at the Richard Rodgers Theater in New York, one of the actors, Brandon Dixon, stepped forward to make a public appeal on behalf of the cast to an elected official in the audience. The official was US Vice President Elect Mike Pence, and the appeal was the following: 'We, sir, we are the diverse Americans who are alarmed and anxious that your new administration will not protect us, our planet, our children, our parents, or defend us and uphold our inalienable rights, sir. But we truly hope that this show has inspired you to uphold our American values and to work on behalf of all of us.' Then, Dixon repeated the final words to emphasize '*all of us*'. The audience in the theatre cheered, but President Elect Donald Trump was quick to decry the action, tweeting that Pence had been 'harassed' and demanding an apology.

'The Theater must always be a safe and special place,' he tweeted, capitalizing the word 'Theater' as though to signal its status as a venerable institution. Yet, we might ask, from what should theatre be safe? Direct address? Political discourse? The discomforts of disagreement and critique? Trump implied that, as a 'special place', theatre should be shielded from the realities of political life and 'safe' from a peaceful act of protest. In contrast, this book aims to show that acts of protest can be among the most moving and significant performances that theatre has to offer. This book is dedicated to those inside and outside the theatre who continue to protest for equality, freedom, and justice for all.

theatre & protest

Introduction

On 21 February 2012, a brief performance that would have a lasting impact took place. Less than a week before Russia's presidential elections in which then Prime Minister Vladimir Putin made his bid for a third term as President, members of the feminist punk performance collective Pussy Riot performed what they called a 'Punk Prayer' in Moscow's imposing Cathedral of Christ the Saviour. Wearing their signature costume of brightly coloured dresses, tights, and balaclavas, they mounted the soleas (a raised platform in front of the iconostasis) and performed a series of choreographed punk rock dance moves while shouting the lyrics of a song asking the Virgin Mary to 'chase Putin away'. Guards almost immediately descended upon the performers, but the group persisted in their action for close to 60 seconds before being escorted from the building. That evening, they posted on YouTube a music video containing footage of the performance, which would go on to be viewed by millions of people worldwide. 'Punk Prayer' would be lauded as both an important act of political protest and a significant piece of performance art. It would earn Pussy Riot a spot on ArtReview's 2012 'Power 100' list of the most influential artists that year.

Russia's response to the performance would also be watched by people around the globe. Investigations into the action began within days, and in March, three members of the band were arrested and held without bail. A criminal trial against them began in late July, and within three weeks all three were convicted of hooliganism motivated by religious hatred and sentenced to two years in prison. The trial was repeatedly described by the women's lawyers and by the press as a 'show trial', a term for a public court case whose outcome has already been determined by the authorities and which is conducted purely as a form of state propaganda. Meanwhile, the accused and their supporters did their best to turn the theatrical nature of the trial to their advantage: when the three arrested women gave testimony in court, passionately decrying the Russian judicial system, their speeches were met with enthusiastic applause in the courtroom. The judge tried to control the crowd, admonishing those present with the words 'we are not in a theatre'. Yet, when the women exited the courtroom, they were given a standing ovation.

Outside the court, objections to the prosecution and conviction of Pussy Riot also frequently took theatrical form. 'Free Pussy Riot!' protestors took to the streets wearing their own brightly coloured dresses and balaclavas. Numerous re-enactments of the 'Punk Prayer' were performed in art and club venues. On the day of the final verdict, London's Royal Court Theatre, a venue long celebrated for presenting challenging new work, re-presented the women's testimonies, translated into English, in a free rehearsed reading as part of a day of global protest in support of the collective. Then, in March 2013, in Moscow, while two members of the group, Nadezhda Tolokonnikova and Maria Alyokhina, remained in prison, Swiss director Milo Rau and the International Institute of Political Murder staged a re-trial of the Pussy Riot case with public figures representing both sides. Included in the production was the third convicted Pussy Riot member, Yekaterina Samutsevich, who had been released in October 2012 following an appeal. The performance was interrupted by immigration authorities who demanded to see Rau's visa, as well as by a group of men in Cossack uniforms and the police. Upon being allowed to continue, the trial reached its conclusion with the jury, composed of members of the Russian public, narrowly acquitting the group.

In the years since Tolokonnikova and Alyokhina were released, Pussy Riot has continued to inspire theatrical responses. In 2015, American playwright Barbara Hammond premiered a new play, *We Are Pussy Riot*, at the Contemporary American Theatre Festival (CATF). The performance began before the house opened with actors recreating the 'Punk Prayer' protest in the lobby of the theatre, complete with actors dressed as policemen to drag them away. Inside the auditorium, the play continued to involve its audience in the action, including bringing audience members on stage to act as witnesses in the trial scene. The CATF advertised the play as a '*revolutionary* experience' (CATF email, 2015, italics in the original). However, the play was also self-conscious about its differences from an act of political protest. As one reviewer noted, 'On several occasions during the play the Pussy Rioters declare that if what we in the audience were watching weren't theatre but a protest, then we'd be outraged, offended, or otherwise emotionally engaged' (Oliver, 2015). When asked in an interview if she was writing the play 'the way Pussy Riot would', Hammond responded, 'No. Pussy Riot wouldn't write a play – Pussy Riot's actions are spontaneous, public and often get them arrested' (Anderson, 2015).

Yet, in June 2016, Alyokhina revealed that she herself was writing her first play, *Burning Doors*, addressing not only Pussy Riot's story but the stories of other imprisoned artists in Russia as well. Significantly, the play, in which Alyokhina would also star, was developed in collaboration with the Belarus Free Theatre – a company that itself must work in secret in its home country after having been banned on political grounds. *Burning Doors* premiered in September 2016 at London's Soho Theatre.

As this series of related events suggests, theatre and protest are often closely interlinked in the contemporary cultural and political landscape. Protest actions frequently take the form of performance, and the line between protest and performance art is often difficult to draw. In addition to Pussy Riot's 'Punk Prayer', one could point to numerous other examples from recent years that blur distinctions between protest and performance art, such as Columbia University art student Emma Sulkowicz's *Mattress Performance (Carry That Weight)* (New York, 2014–2015) or the protest performances of the 'Feminist Five' in China, who, like Pussy Riot, were arrested in 2015 for their actions. At the same time, theatre spaces and theatre productions provide valuable platforms for responding to ongoing political situations, both to galvanize support for particular causes and to stage opposition to perceived injustices. Here, one could place the Royal Court Theatre and International Institute of Political Murder productions in support of Pussy Riot within a long lineage of documentary and verbatim theatre practices, from the Living Newspapers of the 1930s to recent work by groups such as 'iceandfire' in the UK, which create theatre from documents of current events with the aim of intervening in those events as they are happening. Moreover, as Hammond's and Alyokhina's plays demonstrate, theatre can also be inspired by protest and can serve to extend the conversations initiated by protest actions, sustaining interest in these actions and their causes long after the immediate political response has faded from the news. Tim Price's *Protest Song* (National Theatre, London, 2013), which explored the London Occupy movement (2011–2012) from the imagined perspective of a homeless person one year after the protest camp was dismantled, is another example.

However, the relationship between theatre and protest is also an uneasy one. Doubts about theatre's capacity to intervene in the social world abound, especially when it comes to theatre in its most recognized forms, which is to say, theatre that takes place in theatres and names itself as such. Hence, despite Rau's involvement of real opponents in his staging of *The Moscow Trials*, journalist and author Masha Gessen lamented in a *New York Times* post (2013) that the performance remained, disappointingly, a 'simple – and pale – reflection of reality', because, in the end, the acquittal in the theatre 'had no actual consequences'. And, despite *We Are Pussy Riot's* attempts to reproduce the energy of Pussy Riot's protest action, at least one reviewer worried that 'the theatrical bells and whistles ultimately come across as incoherent and self-indulgent, overshadowing the activists' original act of witness' (Wren, 2015). Not just paling in comparison to the reality, but threatening to eclipse it, theatre, this reviewer suggests, might even detract from the gravity of a political situation. As we will see, similar concerns have frequently been expressed in discussions of theatre's political potential.

To explore the relationship between theatre and protest is thus to consider two seemingly opposed stories. It is, on the one hand, to encounter a long history of mutual affinity between the two – a history in which theatre has been used in the service of social and political movements, protests have made use of theatrical forms, and theatre, in turn, has been inspired by political actions. On the other hand, it is to confront persistent mistrust in theatre's ability to *act politically* as well as questions about whether this is even its proper place. This book aims to think through these points of intersection and tension between theatre and protest. What makes theatre and protest such beneficial partners? Why, nevertheless, is there so much scepticism about theatre's ability to have a political impact? Can protest ever happen in the theatre? What does protest offer to theatre? And why is theatre useful to protest? These are some of the questions that I will explore in the following pages.

Contentious performances

In focusing on the relationship between theatre and protest, this book does not attempt to cover all that could be included within the vast realms of 'political theatre' and 'activist performance'. Many forms of theatre and performance – including those developed by Brazilian theatre director and activist Augusto Boal and discussed in his book *Theatre of the Oppressed* (1979), those referred to as 'applied theatre' (which uses techniques of theatre to address issues relevant to specific communities), and other forms of socially engaged performance – have activist aims. However, not all of these involve activities that would be described as 'protest' (though they might contribute to developing the political consciousness that could lead one to protest). This is a good reminder that activism takes many forms, from raising awareness, to teaching and learning new skills, to building and sustaining communities. Rather than attempting to address all of the ways in which activism and theatre come together, this book is interested more specifically in what social movements scholar Charles Tilly termed 'contentious performances'. For Tilly, protest is a form of contentious performance. It involves public actions in which 'actors make claims bearing on someone else's interests, in which governments appear either as targets, initiators of claims, or third parties' (2008, p. 5). Contentious performances involve public expressions of dissent against prevailing systems, and they demand change. Such instances of making claims are contentious, of course, because not everyone shares the same interests. With their 'Punk Prayer', Pussy Riot demonstrated their opposition to Putin's bid for presidency as well as to various church and state policies. In doing so publicly – and in an area of the church reserved for male clergy – they protested against the prevailing interests of church and state, and it is clear that their performance was contentious. Many of Pussy Riot's immediate audience members were not at all sympathetic to their cause, while many who viewed the video subsequently were. Contentious performances are thus performances that address contested issues and whose audiences are consequently fractured.

One of the underlying assumptions of this book is that such performances are productive for society. Protest movements have contributed to many positive advances in modern history, from changes in labour conditions and voting rights to the peaceful overthrow of dictatorships. Yet, protests can also feel inconvenient at times. One of the things they do, after all, is interrupt the usual proceedings of daily life, whether by marching down a city street and forcing traffic diversions, occupying a building and inhibiting 'business as usual', or, as in the case of Pussy Riot, disrupting the conventional rituals of a site with an unexpected (and sometimes unwelcome) performance. As we will see, protest can also seem inconvenient for the theatre, particularly in its institutionalized forms, since protest can disrupt the theatre's usual procedures too. Nevertheless, theatre has an important history of producing contentious performances, and, as I hope to show, the sometimes uncomfortable eruption of contention in the theatre can be valuable, not only politically, but theatrically as well. Finally, it should be said that the notion of contentious performance does not in itself imply any particular political viewpoint. Protest performances are enacted by those on the left and the right of the political spectrum. Furthermore, the politics of any individual use of protest are particular to that context. While most of the work related to theatre and activism emerges from a left-leaning political position, which I share, my aim here is less to convince you of a political viewpoint than to argue that contentious performances are productive, and they can make for good theatre.

In the following section, I offer a brief overview of some key ways in which theatre and protest have come together in the West since the beginning of the twentieth century before moving on to a consideration of some of the major tensions between them. As I will show, while theatre and performance scholars and social movements scholars have long recognized that theatre and protest coincide in various ways, there are, nevertheless, a number of points at which they seem to conflict with one another. These include: *protests against theatre*, where protest would appear to threaten not only an individual production's ability to carry on but also one of theatre's most cherished values, the freedom of expression; *protests by and in theatres*, which have been plagued by doubts about theatre's ability to engage in real political action; and the *theatricalization of protests* in the form of protest re-enactments, where theatricality itself has often been seen as a threat to the legitimacy and urgency of political action. Addressing these trouble spots will be the aim of the remaining sections of the book. For, as a politically committed person who also spends a lot of time in theatres and other performance spaces, I am motivated by a sense that, in addition to affirming the value of political performances outside of theatres, we might also expect theatre, as an art form and a social institution, to serve as a site for the expression of dissent. To make my case, I consider a range of examples from the early part of the twentieth century (just as modern theatre was taking hold) to the present, drawn primarily from Europe and the United States (reflecting my own geographic positioning as a US-born scholar currently living and working in the United Kingdom), with the aim of affirming the productive intersection of theatre and protest precisely at those points where they might otherwise appear to be at odds. I take this relatively broad historical view not to paint a narrative of progress, or to look nostalgically to a past when protest (in or out of the theatre) seemed more possible, but to show that the intersections between theatre and protest are longstanding ones and that the tensions that arise between them are very much connected to developments of modern theatre which continue to shape theatre as an institution today. As my discussion moves back and forth across time, my hope is that readers might be encouraged to look further into theatre and protest histories and that history might prove to be inspiring for those wanting to act politically today.

Convergences and divergences between theatre and protest

Theatre as protest

Without question, theatre has contributed to social and political movements across the twentieth and twenty-first centuries in multiple ways. To begin with, theatre-makers have long devoted their skills to producing plays and other performances in the name of protest. In 1908, the Actresses' Franchise League was founded to support the women's suffrage movement in the UK by staging plays and training suffragettes in the art of public speaking. In the 1920s and 1930s, the Workers' Theatre Movements in the UK and the US, inspired by similar movements in the Soviet Union and Germany, performed agitprop sketches (an overtly political form of performance whose name derives from 'agitation' and 'propaganda') at political demonstrations, outside factories, and in neighbourhood parks to attract and galvanize supporters of working-class struggle. In the 1960s, a veritable explosion of grassroots theatre companies developed in support of the many political movements of the period. In the US, these included: the Free Southern

Theater, which formed in relation to the civil rights movement (two of the founding members were also directors of the Student Nonviolent Coordinating Committee); the San Francisco Mime Troupe, which developed alongside the Free Speech Movement; El Teatro Campesino, which was founded on the picket lines of the United Farm Workers movement; and the Bread and Puppet Theatre, whose giant papier mâché puppets, used in pageants and antiwar actions alike, have become lasting features of political protests to this day. More recently, Eve Ensler's successful play *The Vagina Monologues* (1996–) gave rise to V-Day, an ongoing global movement to end violence against women and girls. The *Lysistrata Project* (2003) staged over 1,000 readings of Aristophanes' antiwar play on the same day in 59 countries to protest the (then) impending US-led invasion of Iraq. And in 2011, Occupy Broadway brought together numerous well-known theatre and performance artists, including the Bread and Puppet Theatre (like the San Francisco Mime Troupe and El Teatro Campesino, still making work), The Living Theatre, and Reverend Billy and the Church of Stop Shopping, for 24 hours of performance in a 'privately-owned public space' in New York's theatre district as part of the Occupy movement.

As all of these examples make clear, theatre, in the form of plays, sketches, and other artistically framed performances, has long been a significant part of protest movements. Importantly, theatre in these contexts has not merely illustrated political issues but has been itself a form of direct political action, enacting and making visible opposition to existing conditions. That theatre *per se* could be a form of protest is something that social movement scholars have also recognized. For instance, in 1973, political science scholar Gene Sharp outlined 198 examples of what he termed 'nonviolent action'. Under the broad heading of 'Protest and Persuasion', he included a subheading for 'Drama and Music', under which he listed 'performances of plays' as well as 'humorous skits'.

At the same time, theatre can also be found in protest beyond the realm of drama and beyond the presentation of plays or skits before knowing audiences. For instance, Sharp included 'guerrilla theatre' not under 'Drama and Music' but under the broad heading 'Methods of Nonviolent Intervention'. 'Guerrilla theatre' is a term often attributed to the San Francisco Mime Troupe, who coined it in the 1960s in response to the writings of Argentine Marxist revolutionary Che Guevara. For the Mime Troupe, the term referred to a theatre that would seek to establish itself as a nonhierarchical collective of people, fully embedded in a community and responsive to that community's needs. Part of meeting such an ideal meant addressing matters of local concern, performing in public spaces such as parks, and performing for free or on a donation only basis (Davis, 1975, pp. 149–55). 'Guerrilla' in this sense meant a grassroots effort operating outside of official channels to wage a 'little war' (a translation of 'guerrilla') against the status quo. More often, however, the term is understood as Sharp defined it, with all of the connotations of a guerrilla *attack*. Here, guerrilla theatre takes the form of 'a skit, dramatic presentation, or similar act [...] often performed as a disruption of [...] normal proceedings of some group or institution' (2012, p. 145). As Sharp notes, such surprise performances often involve parodies of people in power, and they are designed to attract media attention. Pussy Riot's performance, with its unexpected eruption in the church and its parodying of religious gestures such as the sign of the cross, can be seen as an example of guerrilla theatre in this sense.

Numerous other strategies on Sharp's list also draw from theatre, even though they do not claim to be theatre *per se*. 'Mock awards', 'mock elections', and 'mock funerals', for example, all involve elements of theatre, from the use of costumes and props to the delivery of humorous or moving monologues among other things. In recent years, such forms of nonviolent action have risen in visibility under the label 'creative activism'. Activist handbooks such as Andrew Boyd and Dave Oswald Mitchell's edited collection *Beautiful Trouble: A Toolbox for Revolution* (2012) and steirischer herbst and Florian Malzacher's edited collection *Truth Is Concrete: A Handbook for Artistic Strategies in Real Politics* (2014) describe diverse artistic and theatrical protest tactics. These include 'creative petition deliveries', such as the activist group 38 Degrees' 2011 delivery of a petition to save the UK's National Health Service while dressed in doctors' scrubs and carrying the petition on a stretcher; 'identity correction', a tactic of impersonation coined by activist-performers the Yes Men and famously used in 2004 when Andy Bichlbaum pretended to be a Dow Chemical representative and announced on BBC World News that the company would finally take responsibility for the Bhopal disaster; and 'rebel clowning', such as that used by the Clandestine Insurgent Rebel Clown Army, which aims to merge the practice of clowning with direct action to mock and disarm political opponents. In *Tactical Performance: The Theory and Practice of Serious Play* (2016), theatre professor, performer, and activist L.M. Bogad acknowledges that while creative protest is 'different from "legit" theatre', activists making use of such strategies 'can still learn a great deal from that medium'. For example, he notes that theatre practitioners know how to 'earn a moment' by delighting and surprising spectators, and they excel in conveying 'specific and accurate emotion[s]', both of which help to convince and keep the attention of an audience (p. 45). Thus, '"legit" theatre', as Bogad calls it, contributes to protest not only through the production of plays and other performances by dedicated theatre-makers, but also by lending its techniques to artists and activists seeking to provoke spectators through a wide range of creative actions that do not necessarily call themselves theatre.

Protest is theatrical

One reason why theatre and protest work so well together is because, as I've already suggested, protest is *itself* a form of performance. Significantly, this is true not only in those instances where art and activism merge most explicitly, as in 'artistic activism' or even 'artivism'. It is also true of more traditional forms of protest, such as demonstrations, rallies, marches, and occupations, which make use of a wide array of expressive techniques to make their claims.

From the inspiring rhetoric of Martin Luther King Jr's 'I have a dream' speech (Washington DC, 1968), to the moving act of 'dying' in die-ins staged by ACT UP protestors (AIDS Coalition to Unleash Power, New York, 1987–), to the insistent banging of pots and pans in cacerolazo protests from Chile (1971–) to Canada (2012), to the wearing of lingerie by participants in international SlutWalks (2011–), to the donning of Guy Fawkes masks by Occupy protestors worldwide (2011–2012), to the singing of protest songs by South Africa's #FeesMustFall protestors (2015–), protest encompasses a vast range of activities carried out in public before various audiences with the aim of inspiring thoughts and emotions that could lead people towards social change.

Here again, an understanding of theatre is helpful, and this is something that both performance scholars and social movement scholars have recognized. While the field of performance studies has expanded its view to include protest (as well as a wide range of performance forms) alongside theatre, sociologists have also increasingly looked to theatre to understand protest. For instance, in 1992, sociologists Robert Benford and Scott Hunt, perceiving a lack in existing sociological theories, proposed to use a dramaturgical framework for understanding how social movements work. One of the things they recognized was that protest actions are usually scripted, not in the sense of 'rigid texts' that activists must follow, but in the sense of 'guides for collective consciousness and action, guides that are circumspect enough to provide behavioural cues when unanticipated events arise yet sufficiently flexible to allow for improvisation' (p. 38). Such scripts inform the actions that protestors take, whether walking silently with candles in a public vigil or chanting loudly outside of a government office. They also inform the language that movement participants use to speak about their cause, for instance, when talking to the media. Other elements such as dress and demeanour are also often scripted in advance. Consider, for instance, the Greensboro lunch counter sit-ins of 1960, in which black civil rights activists (and subsequently white supporters of the movement) occupied seats at 'whites only' lunch counters to protest against racial segregation. The protestors dressed in formal clothes and remained polite and calm, even in the face of verbal and physical aggression from white segregationists who gathered to threaten and intimidate them. It is widely believed that the civil rights activists' respectable dress and behaviour was a major component in persuading white, middle-class viewers of these actions to support desegregation. As this example shows, the staging of protest actions also often involves attention to site, and many protests are 'site-specific', being performed in symbolically significant or practically relevant places and engaging explicitly with the location in some way.

In order to carry out such performances successfully, protest actions are also frequently rehearsed. As choreographer and dance scholar Susan Leigh Foster explores in relation to the lunch counter sit-ins, ACT UP protests, and the 1999 World Trade Organization protest in Seattle, Washington, the use of civil disobedience in particular requires that activists have 'rehearsed specific procedures of non-cooperation'

(2003, p. 396). Thus, protestors engaging in forms of occupation such as sit-ins, die-ins, or blockades frequently practise such things as locking arms while being jostled and going limp when police begin to drag them away. Far from being spontaneous eruptions, as is often assumed (and as Hammond suggested Pussy Riot's action was), most protests are the outcome of extensive planning and rehearsal.

Theatre and protest are thus intricately connected in a variety of ways. They have intersected historically, through the efforts of overlapping communities of theatre-makers, performance artists, and activists, and formally, through a shared attention to theatrical and performance elements. From 'performances of plays' in support of political movements, to a wide array of 'creative' interventions performed by activists and artists alike, to protest actions that make no claim to being art but require attention to dramaturgy (and, often, just as much inventiveness), theatre and protest have long been fruitful collaborators in creating what Tilly called a 'repertoire of contention'.

The limits of theatre

Yet, despite these many connections, the relationship between theatre and protest is also marked by a common belief that theatre in its more institutionalized forms is hopelessly removed from real political action. Of concern have been both the kinds of theatre that take place in theatre venues and the constraints of those venues themselves.

Significantly, some of the most influential theatre-makers of the twentieth century are those who sought to activate its political potential. The Norwegian playwright Henrik Ibsen, who is often thought of as the 'father' of modern drama and its most prevalent form, realism, transformed the theatre by bringing political concerns to the stage at a time when many believed that theatre was purely for entertainment. For Irish playwright George Bernard Shaw, who was greatly influenced by Ibsen, the most important innovation in Ibsen's plays was the introduction of a discussion, which was meant to continue after the play's end, instead of the usual resolution of conflict that structured the well-made plays of the nineteenth century. Ibsen's *A Doll's House* (1879) is exemplary for Shaw (1958 [1913], p. 171). The discussion is introduced towards the end of the third act. Just when a well-made play would resolve things with a 'happy' ending, as Torvald rejoices that he is now free of the threat of blackmail and therefore ready to forgive his wife (who borrowed money illegally in order to fund a trip to support his health), Nora instructs her husband to sit down, explaining that she has much to talk over with him. She points out that, in eight years of marriage, they have never had a serious conversation. This acknowledgement precipitates one of the most famous – and, at the time, scandalous – endings in theatre history: noting that she has never been asked her opinion about anything, by either her father or her husband, Nora announces her intention to leave her husband and children in order to establish her own views on the world. The play ends with the sound of the door closing behind her as Nora leaves. The heated debates that ensued in Ibsen's time about whether this was an acceptable thing for a woman to do (and the censorship enforced by those who felt it wasn't) are evidence that the discussion that Ibsen initiated through the character of Nora extended well beyond the world of the play.

In his own plays, Shaw sought to develop this element of discussion further by integrating it from the beginning. Rather than presenting a contest between 'clear right and wrong', he aimed to show 'a conflict of unsettled ideals', which would generate debate and new ways of thinking among theatre-goers (p. 176). This is how the socialist Shaw could write a play like *Major Barbara* (1905), in which the apparent hero is a wealthy capitalist and arms manufacturer, while the people who are getting things wrong are the Salvation Army troops trying to help the poor. Rather than allowing his viewers to rest comfortably in their established moral or political outlooks, he sought to inspire a genuine re-evaluation of such ideals.

German playwright and director Bertolt Brecht is another influential theatre-maker of the twentieth century who wanted his audiences to question their pre-existing ideas. Like Ibsen and Shaw, he too wrote 'problem plays' which aimed to encourage audiences to think through challenging social issues in new ways. But Brecht also believed that, in order to do so, it was necessary to depart from the conventions of stage realism. While Brecht commended Shaw in 1926 for recognizing that 'the mere reproduction of reality does not give an impression of truth' and for creating instead characters capable of 'dislocating our stock associations' (1964, p. 11), he argued in 1934 that works by Ibsen and his contemporaries 'remain important historical documents, but they no longer move anybody. A modern spectator can't learn anything from them' (1964, p. 66). In order to move contemporary spectators, Brecht sought to disrupt elements of realist theatre such as the darkened auditorium and the 'fourth wall', which aim to create the illusion that one is observing real people in real situations with whom one is meant to identify. Instead of striving to create such an illusion of reality, he introduced techniques of estrangement (*Verfremdungseffekt* in Brecht's native German) aimed precisely at maintaining spectators' awareness that what they were watching was a *play* about which they should think critically, questioning rather than taking for granted the characters' actions and choices.

In their own ways, all three of these influential theatre-makers sought to critique, or protest against, aspects of their contemporary societies and to use theatre to inspire change. Yet, despite their undeniable impact on *theatre*, their success in turning the theatre into a place for political debate capable of having an impact *beyond* the theatre would be a source of continuing doubt. Theatre critic Robert Brustein, who argued in the 1960s that modern drama as a whole could be understood as a 'theatre of revolt', nevertheless asserted that the revolutionary potential of all three playwrights' work was ultimately confined to the theatre:

> The revolt of the dramatist is more imaginative than practical – imaginative, absolute, and pure. In the earlier phases of the theatre of revolt – in some

of the works of Ibsen, for example, and of Shaw –
the drama sometimes begins to look like an act of
utility; and in the plays of Brecht, it is designed to
lead to political revolution. Even in the majority of
these works, however, the programmatic element
is actually insignificant – or much too radical for
any practical application. (1964, p. 8)

A big part of the problem is that modern theatre, as it
developed as an institution of art and moved away from
'popular' nineteenth-century forms such as melodrama,
became increasingly a bourgeois enterprise, attended by
middle- and upper-class patrons. Concerns about this
emerged early in the twentieth century among those who
were keen to use theatre as a form of political action. For
instance, the Workers' Theatre Movement in the UK was
very much influenced by Shaw, and performed his plays
in the early days of the movement. However, they came
to worry about the relevance of Shaw's plays, which were
written for theatres such as 'the Royal Court in London,
catering to a "concerned" minority of the professional
classes, and more artistically-inclined scions of the bour-
geoisie' (Samuel, MacColl and Cosgrove, 1985, p. xvii).
The Workers' Theatre wanted to reach an audience of
workers themselves, so they began to write their own plays.
In doing so, they looked to other models, particularly to
agitprop, a form considered more accessible to amateurs
and those less familiar with theatre. Similar moves away
from bourgeois forms of theatre towards popular traditions

thought to be able to speak to a wider array of people have been made by many explicitly activist theatre groups (the San Francisco Mime Troupe, for instance, embraced the sixteenth-century Italian form commedia dell'arte).

Another problem with the development of theatre as an institution of art concerns the mode of spectatorship that this theatre encourages. As theatre scholar Christopher Balme argues in *The Theatrical Public Sphere* (2014), the rise of modern drama progressively 'transformed the theatre from a rowdy, potentially explosive gathering into a place of concentrated aesthetic absorption' (p. 3). In prioritizing quiet, focused attention over vocal communicative response from audience members, theatre since that time, Balme argues, 'has become to all intents and purposes a private space' (p. 3). This notion of privacy suggests at least two things: first, that the theatre, as a space where only some members of society gather (those able and willing to pay the ticket price, for instance), is enclosed and separated from the public sphere (not everyone can or does attend the theatre); and second, that in encouraging a contemplative approach to spectatorship, the theatre privileges a private, internal response from its audience members (everyone is meant to have their own experience and not to infringe upon the experience of others). In both ways, theatre as an art form is 'ill-designed for activism or other instrumental ends' (Balme, p. 40).

Importantly, this sense of theatre's limits as an art form housed in a private space affects even the most overtly politicized theatre, including that which takes place in non-commercial theatres and alternative spaces. In 2001, the journal *Theater* asked theatre artists, activists, and scholars, 'How do you make social change?' Lesbian performance artist Holly Hughes – herself well known for her politically provocative performance work, which drew the ire of conservative politicians in the United States a decade earlier in a scandal that was very much about the political impact of performance[1] – lamented:

> Art and politics are considered oil and water, even among the Lefties. Maybe especially among the Lefties. At least the Right thinks that art has power, that art is an agent of social change. Okay, so we are totally destructive, we have sliced, diced, and julienned our nation's moral fiber [...]. But that is better than the standard leftist take on art: art is decadent, bourgeois, just another commodity (Kushner, Hughes et al., p. 73).

It is worth pausing over Hughes' contrast between right-wing politicians who believe that theatre has the power to create change (and therefore seek to censor it) and 'Lefties'

---

[1] Hughes was one of four performance artists whose National Endowment for the Arts grants were vetoed by the chairman, John Frohnmayer, in 1990, despite having been selected for the awards by a panel of experts. A high profile court case followed, which was ultimately settled out of court in favour of the artists. The four artists – Holly Hughes, Karen Finley, Tim Miller, and John Fleck – would come to be known as the 'NEA Four'.

who consider theatre to be a bourgeois commodity. This contrast highlights an important irony: that the notion of theatre as a private space, separated from the public sphere and therefore unable to act in relation to it, arises precisely in contexts in which the freedom of expression is taken for granted. As Balme writes, the very 'degree of "licence" permitted on Western European stages' correlates with a conception of theatre as 'a largely private space, an intimate sphere for activities between consenting adults' (p. 17). Conversely, where there is censorship (as Hughes herself experienced), there is 'a deep conviction about the political potency of the theatrical gathering' (Balme, p. 16). Certainly, this is something understood very well by theatre-makers such as the Belarus Free Theatre and anyone working within a context where theatre is regularly censored. Thus, the perceived political potential of even the most contentious performance exists in an inverse relation to the extent that freedom of expression is protected within the theatre. (A similar defanging of protest occurs the more that protest itself is contained within 'protected' designated spaces.)

As it turns out, the perspectives of those who believe in the power of theatre as a form of political action and those who believe that theatre, as an institution, is insulated and ultimately unable to intervene in real politics have more in common than might at first appear. In fact, activist theatre-makers have long argued that, to be politically relevant, theatre needs to *leave the theatre*. This sentiment has been particularly powerful since the 1960s (though, as

we have seen, earlier groups such as the Workers' Theatre
Movement had the same impulse). The Austrian playwright
and novelist Peter Handke's 1969 text 'Theater-in-the-Street
and Theater-in-Theaters' is instructive. Declaring the
impotence of Brecht's conception of political theatre in particular, Handke argues that, while he agrees with Brecht's
politics, he disagrees that political solutions could be proposed in a play: 'I myself would support Marxism every
time as the only possible solution to our governing problems,' he writes, 'but not its proclamation in a play, in the
theatre' (p. 9). To show why, he proposes the absurdity of
any kind of protest action taking place in a theatre: 'That is
just as false and untrue as chanting slogans for the freedom
of Vietnam when this chanting takes place in the *theatre*;
or when, as in Oberhausen recently, "genuine" coal miners
appeared in the *theatre* and struck up a protest song' (p. 9,
italics in the original). Here, we encounter another perceived limitation of theatre as an art form: its association
with artifice. Suggesting that any kind of protest action in
a theatre would be void of truth, and therefore of effect,
Handke asserts that 'committed theatre these days doesn't
happen in theatres (those falsifying domains of art where
every word and movement is emptied of significance)'
(p. 9). Rather, he argues, it takes place in the streets and
other non-theatre spaces such as lecture halls, churches,
and department stores. Such a position has held sway in
theatre and performance circles for many years. (A similar
approach informs theatre and performance studies scholar
Baz Kershaw's *The Radical in Performance: Between Brecht and*

Baudrillard (1999), where Kershaw argues against 'political theatre' in favor of a 'radical performance' that goes 'beyond theatre' (p. 16).)

The limits of protest

At the same time, the sense that theatre (in theatres) and protest are incompatible with one another also arises from another direction: not from those who worry about theatre-as-art's limited ability to affect the public sphere, but from those keen to *protect* theatre's artistic merits from the perceived limits of political action. In this view, theatre – including 'political theatre' – is thought to require more nuance than direct political action is presumed to have. Otherwise, it risks being mere 'propaganda'. For example, in his acceptance speech for the Nobel Prize in 2005, English playwright Harold Pinter used the opportunity to take a political stand against the United States' foreign policy and its propagation of lies leading to the Iraq War. Yet, while Pinter insisted upon citizens' obligation to seek out the truth in the face of political lies, he nevertheless asserted that the 'truths' of theatre are necessarily more complex and contradictory: '[T]here never is any such thing as one truth to be found in dramatic art. There are many. These truths challenge each other, recoil from each other, reflect each other, ignore each other, tease each other, are blind to each other,' he said. Discussing the possibility of political theatre, Pinter opined that 'characters must be allowed to breathe their own air. The author cannot confine and constrict them to satisfy his own taste or disposition or prejudice.' Above all, he warned that 'sermonizing has to be avoided at all cost'. With these words, Pinter repeated familiar arguments against theatre with political aims; Shaw had already acknowledged and resisted the assumption that people did not want to be 'preached at in the theatre' (1958 [1913], p. 143). Even in the midst of an impassioned political speech, Pinter fell back on long-established views that the best art is free of overt political agendas and open to multiple interpretations.

Such values are also connected to the idea that 'great art' transcends its historical moment. As American playwright Tony Kushner writes in the same *Theater* survey as Hughes, critiquing the normative values of critics, 'a play that explores human behavior and *rescues it* from the political and historical, which confirms its condition as eternal, essential, unchangeable, is, it is assumed, going to be entertaining to people a thousand years hence' (Kushner, Hughes et al., p. 63, emphasis added). Criticizing such an approach, and linking it to the commodification of theatre-as-art, Kushner comments sarcastically that such plays are prized because 'after a thousand years of appreciation, their market value will be immense!' (p. 63). In contrast, much overtly activist theatre and performance aims to respond directly to present circumstances. This also means that it may be devised quickly and produced without all of the resources that can make theatre so impressive as an art form. Even those who have great respect for activist forms of theatre, such as agitprop, acknowledge that such work is often amateur. Thus, while political theatre (in theatres) has long been accused of being 'bad activism', overtly activist theatre and performance have often been dismissed as 'bad art' from which 'good theatre' needs to distinguish itself.

In the following pages, I aim to challenge such distinctions between theatre and protest by looking closely at three areas where theatre and protest would appear to be most at odds. One of the things I hope to show is that not only does protest have something to learn from theatre, as Bogad suggests, but that theatre has something to learn from protest, too – even, I will argue, from protests against it. Second, I want to challenge Handke's claim that people chanting antiwar slogans or 'genuine' activists singing a protest song *in the theatre* are always 'false and untrue'. Looking at examples where precisely such things have happened, I explore the possibility for political action to take place within the theatre. Throughout, one of my goals is to convince you that theatre may in fact become 'good art' – which is to say, formally innovative and exciting art – precisely at the point that it intersects with protest. Finally, I also hope to show that the art (or, for some, the artifice) of theatre is not a threat to legitimate protest but can serve to extend its reach.

Protesting theatre

In the street

There is perhaps no greater point of tension between theatre and protest than in protests against theatre productions. After all, the aim of such protests is often to bring about the production's closure. When violent, as in the case of protests against British Sikh playwright Gurpreet Kaur Bhatti's play *Behzti* (*Dishonour*) at the Birmingham Repertory Theatre in 2004, protests can pose a genuine threat to the safety of theatre-makers and theatre-goers alike. (Bhatti received death threats and the Birmingham Rep sustained thousands of pounds in damage.) Yet, peaceful protest can also be an important way of engaging with theatre, even if it is not what most theatre-makers would choose. In this section, I consider the challenges posed by protests against theatre productions and suggest some ways in which such protests might also enrich theatre itself.

Here is an example that I experienced first-hand. It was an unusually warm September evening in London in 2014. I was on my way to the opening night of a production that was already steeped in acclaim and controversy. *Exhibit B* (2010), by white South African artist Brett Bailey, had already toured a number of European cities. Most recently, it had been staged at the Edinburgh International Festival, where respected *Guardian* critic Lyn Gardner gave it a five star review. The Barbican art centre's description of the production (programmed in the edgier space of the Waterloo Vaults) began with a quote from acclaimed theatre director Peter Brook lauding *Exhibit B* as 'an extraordinary achievement'. Yet, criticism of the piece had also been widely publicized. The performance had sparked protests in Berlin in 2012 and was deemed 'Edinburgh's most controversial show' (O'Mahony, 2014). For the London production, an online petition had accumulated over 20,000 signatures calling for the Barbican to withdraw the piece, and hundreds of people had gathered outside of the Barbican prior to the opening to protest the show.

The performance (which is still on tour as I write) takes the form of a series of tableaux vivants, or 'living pictures', in which performers, all of whom identify as black, pose silently in scenes depicting atrocities committed by European powers against African people from the seventeenth century to the present. The scenes reference abuses including: the display of Angelo Soliman's stuffed corpse in the Imperial Library in Vienna in the late 1700s; the exhibition of Sarah (Saartjie) Baartman under the name 'Hottentot Venus' in freak shows in Europe in the early nineteenth century; the brutal practice known as 'red rubber', in which native people in the Belgian Congo were forced to collect rubber under constant (and frequently imposed) threat of death in the late nineteenth century; the Herero and Namaqua genocide carried out by the German Empire in the early twentieth century; and the contemporary plight of African migrants and asylum seekers, a number of whom have died during forced deportations from Europe. The performers are almost entirely cast anew in each city the tour visits; only a quartet of Namibian singers remains constantly with the show. All performers are instructed by Bailey to remain still during 100-minute sessions and to make eye contact with spectators, who are also instructed to remain silent as they move through the exhibit.

This, at least, is what I understand from others' reviews and descriptions of the piece. I didn't end up seeing it myself. Instead, as I exited Waterloo Station, on my way to my

8:50 pm timeslot, I received a call that the show had been cancelled in response to the protest against it. Citing the 'extreme nature of the protest', the Barbican asserted that it 'had no choice' but to call off the run (Barbican Press Release, 2014).

The protest against *Exhibit B* emerged from a Change.org petition initiated by Sara Myers. Of primary concern to the protestors was the form of the production, which replicates histories of colonial display of African people and other non-Europeans before curious white European and American audiences in a variety of practices (including popular freak shows, ethnographic displays, and scientific investigations) collectively referred to as 'human zoos'. For Bailey, *Exhibit B* intends to function as a 'critique of human zoos and the objectifying, dehumanising colonial/racist gaze' (Third World Bunfight website). According to him, the performers looking back at spectators unsettle this gaze and its attendant objectification, which, the exhibition suggests, in its linking of historical and contemporary injustices, continues today. However, for the protestors, the production's very placing of silenced black bodies on display at the bidding of a white director before largely white audiences *reinforced* rather than critiqued these dynamics, and continued rather than departed from practices of objectification. They charged Bailey and the Barbican with 'using black bodies and the bloody history of white supremacism' to generate sales and attention, rather than presenting a genuine challenge to this history (Myers, 2014).

In the aftermath of the Barbican's decision to close the production, the performance and the protests against it were hotly debated in the media and other online forums. These discussions largely pitted the protestors *against* the theatre – not just the Barbican, but the theatre more broadly. The protestors were repeatedly accused of 'mob censorship'. The press release from the Barbican portrayed the protestors as presenting a 'serious threat to the safety of performers, audiences and staff' and stated, 'We find it profoundly troubling that such methods have been used to silence artists and performers and that audiences have been denied the opportunity to see this important work.' It concluded by repeating that the Barbican was 'disturbed at the potential implications this silencing of artists and performers has for freedom of expression', thus positioning the protestors as a danger to one of the most cherished values of the theatre establishment.

Notably, it was the right to present and view difficult art that is itself potentially contentious that those who denounced the protestors sought to defend. Bailey himself asserted, 'I work in difficult and contested territory that is fraught with deep pain, anger and hatred. There are no clear paths through this territory, and it is littered with landmines' (Bailey, 2014). Meanwhile, the protestors' own contentious display was frequently dismissed as simplistic and lacking in nuance. The protestors were repeatedly described as misunderstanding the work in the most basic of ways and not recognizing the difference between a representation of racism and a racist representation. One letter to the *Guardian* suggested that the protestors suffered from a 'failure to distinguish between historical facts on the one hand, and an imaginative response to them on the other' (Parsons, 2014). Whereas Bailey and his defenders argued for *Exhibit B*'s openness to multiple interpretations, the protestors were seen as imputing one, facile reading while denying the possibility for others to generate their own interpretations.

Such characterizations placed the protestors in opposition to the world of theatre – a world that implicitly needs to be defended as a site where potentially controversial ideas can be explored without fear of censorship. No one who truly valued the theatre or recognized its importance as a site of social and political critique, this logic implies, would ever strive to shut down a performance. At the same time, in positioning the protestors as wholly *outside* the theatre, and as threats to the theatre's freedom of expression, the pervasive discourse around the protests accorded with Balme's view that 'most theatre spectators and advocates of artistic freedom privatize theatrical space in order to enjoy this freedom' (p. 167). Implicit in this privatization is the sense that not everyone is invited in. As Balme writes in relation to another theatre piece that sparked protests in Paris in 2011, Romeo Castellucci's *On the Concept of the Face, Regarding the Son of God* (which was protested against by fundamentalist Christian groups who accused it of blasphemy), 'The idea of a self-satisfied, art-enjoying theatre public, which pursues its constitutionally protected right to view performances of a [controversial] nature in the privacy of its publicly subsidized institutions poses anew the question of the public nature of theatre' (p. 167). As those outside the

Waterloo Vaults protested that *Exhibit B* (re)produced harmful scenes of racist oppression, they raised the question of who is included within the theatre's public.

Within the theatrical landscape

In contrast to the pervasive view of the protestors as censoring or 'silencing' Bailey or *Exhibit B*, I suggest that the protestors raised legitimate questions about who was included in this piece (as creators, performers, and viewers) and whose voices it enabled to be heard. In objecting to the performance's staging of silent black bodies before a presumptively white audience (Bailey's own comments about the piece suggest that it aims to confront an implicitly white European audience with the atrocities committed by Europeans against black African people), the protestors acted not from a failure to understand the difference between real life and theatrical representation, but from a recognition that performances in the theatre both enact power relations and influence how people see the world. In charging the Barbican with institutional racism in its programming, they also pointed out that not everyone has as much 'freedom' of expression, since not everyone has access to the same platforms – in this case a major theatre venue in London. Realizing this means recognizing that, far from being 'free', speech in the theatre is a scarce resource apportioned by and to a few.

Rather than seeing the protestors as *opposed* to the theatre, we might see them as engaging deeply with it and, as Caoimhe Mader McGuinness argues in her discussion of the controversy, as 'claiming their space as legitimate actors in London's theatrical landscape' (2016, p. 213). Refusing to allow the word 'provocative' – as *Exhibit B* has been called repeatedly – to become a mere buzzword or selling point, the protestors insisted that such provocation must lead to dialogue and change.

My own experience of the protest suggested as much. When I arrived with my companions at the tunnel that houses the Vaults performance space under Waterloo Station, there were more police in high-vis vests than protestors, who, we were told by one of the officers, had been dispersed. When we approached closer to the entrance of the venue, we were told that we should leave the area for our own safety. The implication was that the protestors were a menace to us as potential audience members. Instead of departing, however, we struck up a conversation with some of the protestors about why they were protesting. The conversation was wide-ranging. Together, we discussed questions of form, including the stillness of the performers and the use of eye contact. We considered the casting of only black performers as well as the actors' agency in choosing to be part of the production (a number of the performers publicly supported the production in written statements, while others expressed their ambivalence). We reflected on who was most likely to be in the audience for a show presented by the Barbican and what might motivate people to see it. We also discussed the matter of profit and who was financially benefiting from this performance. We talked, in other words, about issues of concern to people who think deeply about theatre and its politics.

Though, at the end of our conversation, disagreements still remained about whether the show should have been allowed to continue, what was clear is that *all* of us were convinced of theatre's importance and invested in its politics. Moreover, what everyone agreed about as we parted amiably was that this was one of the most constructive conversations we had ever had with a group of strangers at a theatre.

Although it may have seemed opposed to the performance, it was the protest that gave rise to this meaningful conversation about *Exhibit B*. We might ask then, could protest against the theatre ever be a productive contribution to it? What would it mean to see protest not as a threat to the theatre but as a legitimate way of engaging with it? Could theatre respond differently to protests against it, neither cancelling the production nor, as happens more frequently, evicting protestors as quickly as possible? Such evictions are almost always justified in the name of protecting free speech: protests are shut down in order to allow the performance to go on. Yet, in doing so, the theatre – including the contemporary avant-garde theatre with all of its intention to provoke – also demonstrates that it is unable to accommodate dissent. For instance, the Christian protestors of Castellucci's *On the Concept of the Face, Regarding the Son of God*, which I mentioned above, interrupted the performance one evening by mounting the stage and displaying a banner calling for an end to 'Christianophobia'. (They objected, among other things, to the desecration of a huge portrait of the face of Christ during the performance.) They used well-established peaceful protest tactics: in addition to the banner, they vocalized their opposition, and, upon attempts by theatre staff, performers, and even audience members to disperse them, they locked arms, knelt down, and sang. However, the protest was stopped within a few minutes as police arrived and arrested the protestors. While I would argue against the Christian protestors' claims of oppression given the pervasive influence of Christianity in secular Western societies (making Castellucci's controversial engagement with the image of Christ more the minority than the rule), I agree with performance scholar Sandra D'Urso that it is worth questioning the principle of using the police in the theatre to evict peaceful protestors. For, regardless of one's political viewpoint, 'what ensued was something that in the end looked much more like a scenography of the police state [...] than like a democratic reckoning with dissent' (D'Urso, 2013, p. 43).

Inside the auditorium

What could it mean to admit protest into the theatre? To imagine this, let us go back to the early days of modern theatre. As Neil Blackadder explores in his book *Performing Opposition: Modern Theater and the Scandalized Audience* (2003), protests by audience members in the theatre were in fact a relatively common occurrence at the end of the nineteenth century and the beginning of the twentieth century, as modern drama was emerging. Blackadder argues that protests at this time were a response against the increasing passivity of the audience, which coincided with the theatre's transformation into a 'private' bourgeois institution. As he notes, prior to this period, 'demonstrative expression of disapproval or approval by theater audiences was customary' (p. xi). However, as the nineteenth century wore on, spectators increasingly 'sat quietly in the dark, not applauding, let alone speaking or shouting, until the end of the performance' (p. xi). Protests against plays in this period were thus acts of resistance against this new form of spectatorship, which separated audiences from what was happening on stage and prevented them from interjecting or expressing their opinions about it. Opposition to a theatre that allows only for silent approval (or silent disapproval – in the silence, the distinction is difficult to detect) therefore accompanied modern theatre's emergence from the start.

One difference with protests in this earlier period is that the immediate expulsion of protestors from the theatre was not yet a given. Take for example the 'Playboy Riots', which occurred in response to Irish playwright J.M. Synge's *The Playboy of the Western World* at the Abbey Theatre in Dublin in 1907. As in the cases of *Exhibit B* and *On the Concept of the Face*, the protestors against Synge's play objected to a representation that they felt did harm to a group with whom they identified: in this case the Irish villagers who, in Synge's play, first celebrate the arrival of an apparent murderer in their midst and then violently attack him later in the play after his tale of patricide is revealed to have been a lie. As Blackadder recounts, the protestors objected that *The Playboy*, with its crude language and suggestive references to women in 'shifts', did not paint a fair picture of life in rural Ireland. 'This is not Irish life!' they called out during the production, amidst booing, hissing, and stamping their feet (p. 76).

Importantly, two things did *not* happen: although the protestors called for the play to be cancelled, it was not; and nor was the protest immediately shut down. Rather, in what Lady Gregory (who was one of the co-founders of the Abbey Theatre) would describe, in terms reminiscent of more recent events, as 'a definite fight for freedom from mob censorship', the company continued to perform the play throughout its week-long run (Blackadder, p. 89). At the same time, though the theatre did call in police starting on the second night to maintain order in the theatre and some arrests were made for 'offensive behavior', the protests as a whole continued for several nights. Theatre and protest thus both carried on in a way that seems much less likely today.

Although the notion of a 'riot' suggests a spontaneous eruption, the protests at the Abbey were both more premeditated and less violent than that term implies. While spectators on the opening night did not know what to expect, it is clear that a number of people who had objected on the opening night returned on subsequent nights along with new objectors who came to express their opposition. Raising their voices, stamping their feet, and even playing trumpets brought into the theatre expressly for the purpose of disrupting the performance, they mounted a raucous counter-performance designed to drown out the stage production (Blackadder, p. 83). They largely succeeded: although the actors carried on, they were frequently reduced to miming the actions wordlessly in the face of the vociferous opposition.

The theatre directors tried several methods to quell the protests. On the second night, William Fay, another co-founder of the theatre and the lead actor and director of this production, halted the performance and offered the protestors their money back if they did not like the play, but the protestors responded that they did not want the money (Blackadder, p. 79). In declining to have their ticket price refunded, they insisted that a theatrical production was more than a commodity to be returned to the vendor if it does not meet expectations. Refusing to be cast as dissatisfied customers, they insisted instead that a production mounted by the Irish National Theatre Society should be in dialogue with them. Although the theatre, in making its case against arrested protestors, would subsequently cast the protestors as 'intruders' who were not regular attendees at the theatre, many of the protestors were in fact regular audience members (Blackadder, p. 98), and they demanded that their position should be heard.

On the third night of the performance, William Butler Yeats, another co-founder of the theatre, conceded to the opposition by inviting audience members to a debate the following week. In exchange, he asked for quiet, insisting that 'every man [sic] has a right to hear and condemn it as he pleases, but no man [sic] has a right to interfere with another man [sic] who wants to hear the play' (Blackadder, p. 82). Here, we encounter a corollary to the notion of freedom of expression: the idea of freedom of reception. After all, the problem with censorship is not just that certain voices are silenced, but also that others are deprived of the opportunity to hear those voices. Yet, as with expression, reception is rarely 'free' in the theatre. The protestors were mostly seated in the cheap seats in the pit at the back of the auditorium of the national theatre, and what they objected to was 'the unflattering depiction of rural Ireland in a theatre run largely by Anglo-Irish intellectuals' (Blackadder, p. 89). Given that both the platform for expression and the best seats for reception were controlled by a privileged few, the protestors' refusal to quiet down served to produce a different performance in the theatre – one that the protestors would not otherwise have been able to stage at the Abbey – where a struggle over the representation of an Irish national identity was waged. It seems fair to say that the debate that the theatre organized the following week is not likely to have occurred without this counter-performance.

By the end of the run, the protests abated, and *The Playboy of the Western World* would go on to be considered a classic of the Irish theatre canon (though not without sparking some further, though less vociferous, protests in other places to which it travelled). It could seem that the protestors lost their battle. Yet, the protestors made their opposition to the play known in a way that has come to be inextricably linked to it. *The Playboy* is as famous for the 'riots' that it caused as for the play itself. Moreover, each time it is remounted, it becomes an occasion to reconsider the issues that the protestors raised; programmes and reviews inevitably remind audiences and readers about the riots and open up the question once again, why did Irish nationalists at this moment object to this representation? Arguably, the dynamic interplay between protestors and performance enriched this play.

Theatre's capacity to represent contested ideas is widely valued. Yet, what each of these examples shows is that accommodating dissent within the theatre is not easy. Nevertheless, allowing expressions of opposition in the theatre – even when such expressions are inconvenient – might contribute to theatre's ongoing relevance. (Certainly, recent #WakingTheFeminists protests at the Abbey Theatre represent a demand from those *inside* the institution that the theatre continue to develop its relevance to all members of its public.) Rather than condemning those who protest against the theatre, the theatre might do well to invite the protestors in.

Theatre protests

Rallying the audience

If the theatre productions discussed in the previous section incited protests against them, this is because they were themselves political performances that explicitly addressed problematic social matters and aimed to challenge their audiences' assumptions. Nevertheless, they each struggled to reconcile themselves with the political actions of audiences in response to them. In this section, I explore attempts by theatre-makers themselves to harness theatre's capacity to inspire protest. What happens when protest is enacted *by* the theatre? Can it have any efficacy? Can it be good art?

I turn to another protest taking place in a theatre the same year as the 'Playboy Riots'. This protest was part of Elizabeth Robins' *Votes for Women! A Dramatic Tract in Three Acts* (1907), staged at London's Royal Court Theatre (then, the Court Theatre). Described by the title as a political treatise in dramatic form, *Votes for Women!* was the first suffragette play, and it is credited with having inspired the development of the Actresses' Franchise League the following year. The play depicts the political awakening of a young heiress, Beatrice Dunbarton, after she meets the independent suffragette Vida Levering at a party. The major turning point in the narrative comes in Act II, when Beatrice goes to hear Vida speak at a suffragette rally in London's Trafalgar Square. Beatrice is so moved by the experience that she is persuaded to join the cause, and she subsequently helps to convince her fiancé, a Conservative Member of Parliament, to support the suffrage campaign as well.

Votes for Women! was criticized by some for its use of melodramatic plot conventions at a time when realism was taking hold as the most respected stage form (something Robins herself was well aware of and played an important part in as the first English Hedda Gabler and a champion of Ibsen's work). However, the Trafalgar Square rally, which comprised the second act, was widely acclaimed as both a triumph of stage realism and a tour de force of political theatre. It was lauded by the *Sunday Times* as the 'most brilliant piece of stage-management we have ever had in an English playhouse' (quoted in McDonald, 1995, p. 139). The *Sketch* described it as 'the finest stage crowd scene that has been seen for years' (quoted in Ellis, 2003). The *Observer* called it 'a marvel of verisimilitude' (ibid.). In addition, the scene was attributed real political power: 'The second act may have an influence on social and political life such as no other play has had in this generation,' one reviewer wrote (quoted in McDonald, p. 141).

What was so exciting about Act II was the way it turned the performance in the Court Theatre into a genuine suffrage rally. As an active member of the Women's Social and Political Union (WSPU), Robins had attended many political rallies, and she had given her first speech at one in 1906. As a talented writer, she also wrote many persuasive letters in support of the cause. The speeches in Act II, by an anonymous working woman, a character named Ernestine Blunt (based upon the suffragette Teresa Billington-Greig), a working man, and Vida Levering, each address issues that were relevant to the movement at the time, including the plight of working women and the need for cross-class alliances, the reasons why men ought to support the cause, and concerns around motherhood. The speeches were thus fully engaged with the arguments of the movement. Delivered to a contemporary audience, they were, quite simply, real suffragette speeches.

Moreover, the act was exhilarating because of its creation of a realistic crowd scene. As Jan McDonald (1995) details, it was a feat of ensemble acting because of the interjections of over 20 named characters who formed part of the assembled crowd, and who represented a wide cross-section of society. These characters gave voice to prevailing opinions and attacks against the suffragettes and provided the opportunity for the speakers on the platform to respond with persuasive arguments, lending a 'live' and lively sensibility to the scene. Even more important to the electrifying realism of the scene was how the audience in the theatre was incorporated into it. The stage at the Court Theatre was small (as St. John Hankin wrote in a review for *The Academy* (1907, p. 370), 'about the dimensions of a pocket handkerchief') and therefore unable to hold the crowd of several hundred called for in the stage directions. Harley Granville Barker, who directed the play, addressed this limitation by having the onstage crowd stand with their backs to the audience. The light plot indicated that the speakers should be brightly lit while all lights were to be kept off the crowd (McDonald, p. 143). In this way, attention was drawn towards the suffragette speakers while the onstage crowd blended in with the theatre audience so that *all* became active spectators of the suffragette speeches.

The audience was thus drawn into the scene and made a vital part of it. As Hankin wrote in *The Academy*:

> Mr Barker got over the difficulty [of staging a crowd scene on a small stage] by making *us* his crowd. [...] The crowd on the stage itself was merely a thin line of supers facing the speakers and with their backs to the house. Behind the supers were We. WE were the real crowd and

it was to US that the speeches from the plinth were addressed. We, it was, who, sometimes following the stage crowd and sometimes leading it, laughed or cheered or dissented, as orator after orator harangued us on Women's Rights and Woman's Wrongs. (p. 370, italics and capitalization in original)

By inviting vocal responses from the audience – and allowing for both agreement and disagreement – Act II involved its spectators in a riveting and realistic experience of a suffrage rally. And it did so both for members of the audience who were very familiar with such events (the audience at the opening performance included numerous suffragettes, among them Emmeline and Christabel Pankhurst, on whom Vida Levering's character was reportedly based) and for audience members who may never have gone to such a rally outside the theatre. Thus, the political awakening represented onstage through the character of Beatrice Dunbarton was one that those in the audience who were curious but not yet personally involved may have experienced as well.

Importantly, *Votes For Women!* achieved these effects through formal innovations that challenged the current conventions of stage realism, which separated the audience from the representation by a 'fourth wall'. The play's explicit attempt to act politically was therefore theatrically inventive as well, resulting in a scene that 'caused the greatest interest in theatrical circles' (*Sketch* review quoted in McDonald, p. 146).

Inspiring dissent

Such innovative attempts to turn the theatre into a site for protest can be found at other points in history as well. Consider *Slave Ship: A Historical Pageant* (1967) by Amiri Baraka (aka LeRoi Jones). The play explores African American history in a progression of scenes that moves from the intolerable situation of Africans aboard slave ships, to a failed plantation revolt, to the civil rights movement, and ultimately to the rise of Black Power. It concludes with a call to black audience members to literally stand up from their seats and join the dance that concludes the play, prefiguring the hoped for success of the movement in overcoming white supremacy. As a play addressing the history of African American oppression by a writer who was influenced by Black Power politics, *Slave Ship* had overt political aims and strong theatrical ambitions.

As with *Votes for Women!*, the two came together in immersive staging techniques. The set, designed by Eugene Lee for the Chelsea Theater Center production at the Brooklyn Academy of Music in 1969, turned the entire auditorium into a slave ship. The audience sat crammed together on uncomfortable wooden benches on four sides, with action taking place all around them. Audience members were positioned as though in the hold of the ship, one level up from the tortured human cargo below, whom the audience had to lean forward awkwardly to see in the first movement of the play. Above them, on the deck of the ship, the sailors, the plantation owners, and those with power stomped about on wooden planks that produced part of the soundscape of the piece. African drums, 'hideous screams', chains, and cracking whips also formed the aural environment for a significant part of the opening of the play (*New York Times* reviewer Walter Kerr reported that it was 25 minutes before the first word was spoken, and another 15 minutes before the next). Meanwhile, smells filled the auditorium. Baraka's stage directions indicate: 'Burn incense, but make a significant, almost stifling, smell come up. Pee. Shit. Death.' The audience was thus enveloped within a sensory experience of the horrors of slavery – horrors that the play indicated, through its constant setting aboard the slave ship, continued to shape race relations in the present.

In immersing spectators within this uncomfortable encounter with history, *Slave Ship* aimed to impress upon them the unacceptable reality of this history and to politicize them to act out against it in a revolution that the play encouraged spectators to rehearse for in the final moments of the performance. The techniques used reflected the influence of other experimental theatre-makers, including Antonin Artaud's 'Theatre of Cruelty', Jerzy Grotowski's 'Poor Theatre', and Richard Schechner's 'Environmental Theatre', but they were also received as inventive and new. As Martin Gottfried wrote in the *New York Times* (1971), '"Slave Ship" – the kind of play it is and the way it was done – was just a different kind of theatre.' Among other accolades, the director Gilbert Moses won an Obie award for the production.

For *New York Times* reviewer Clive Barnes, like the reviewers who praised *Votes for Women!* for its verisimilitude, the 1969 production of *Slave Ship*'s success at creating a sense of political urgency in the theatre was connected to its 'emphatically realistic staging'. As with the political speeches in *Votes for Women!*, which were so effective because they were indistinguishable from actual suffragette speeches, *Slave Ship*'s realism may also have come from a sense that the performers were themselves *really* activists. As theatre scholar Harry Elam explains, Moses believed that in order to move audiences to participate, the actors themselves had to be genuinely committed to black liberation politics (1996, p. 17). Thus, while the performers were professional actors rather than activists to begin with, a major part of their rehearsals involved consciousness-raising sessions focusing on African and African American history and the philosophies of the Black Power movement. More than just helping the actors to get into their roles, this training enabled them to see their participation in the production as itself a form of activism.

If *Slave Ship* bore some similarities to *Votes for Women!* in its attempt to immerse spectators in an encounter with real activism, its final scene also differed from the Trafalgar Square scene in important ways. Though *Slave Ship* as a whole was lauded as an innovative piece of theatre, its concluding moments fractured audiences. The play ends with the performers rising up from the condition of slavery (in the Chelsea Theater production, they literally came up through the floor of the slave ship), singing 'Rise, Rise, Rise / Cut these ties, Black Man Rise [...].' In a stylized performance of revolution, while dancing what Baraka describes as 'a new-old dance, Boogalooyoruba line' (a combination of Yoruba African dance and the boogaloo), they kill the 'white voice' that has represented power throughout the play, but not before they also kill a black preacher figure who has been negotiating with the white voice – a figure who would have inevitably evoked Martin Luther King Jr for the audience in 1969. Thus, the play clearly critiques the civil rights movement's emphasis on integration. Upon the final death cry of the 'white voice', the performers in the Chelsea production, resuming their dance and song, reached out to black audience members exclusively (who comprised 60 to 70 per cent of the audience, a high percentage for a theatre such as the Chelsea (Gottfried)) and invited them onto the stage to join the dance and the movement. Lest the dancing seem too celebratory, however, the performance ended with the preacher's head being thrown into the middle of the stage as a stark reminder that the revolution had not yet taken place.

In reaching out solely to black audience members, *Slave Ship* made clear its commitment to Black Power politics. At the same time, so moved by the performance were many white audience members that they also attempted to stand and join the singing and dancing (Elam, 1996, p. 23). However, the invitation was clearly not for them. As Nigerian playwright Wole Soyinka recounts of the impressions of one white critic, 'He, in spite of [his] feelings of identification which had been fed into him from the universality of suffering, found that his emotive identification existed only for him and was not necessarily reciprocal in itself with the essential truths of the evening' (quoted in

Elam, pp. 23–24). The play thus concluded by potentially alienating a significant portion of its audience. (Barnes, for instance, clearly admired the play both as a work of art and as a means of politics, but nevertheless admitted that the play's ending, when 'whitey is got', scared him. 'I am whitey,' he acknowledged.) At the same time, in risking this alienation, the performance may have allowed for real dissent to be experienced in the theatre. Through its affecting rendering of human suffering combined with its refusal to engage in a fiction of a communal solidarity among the audience, the production may have encouraged *all* audience members to consider their own role in overcoming racism differently. While black audience members were invited to join together through a shared history of oppression, white audience members who wanted to act out against racial oppression were forced to acknowledge their own privileged position in relation to it and possibly, in being excluded from the action in the theatre, to take responsibility for acting outside of the theatre in the many situations where their own comfort and identification were unquestioned.

While it is always difficult to point to the direct political effects of any piece of theatre, or protest for that matter, one thing that the New York production of *Slave Ship* does appear to have done was to inspire public discourse on the politics of New York's theatre scene and *its* inclusions and exclusions. The *New York Times* published a 'black view' of the performance by Clayton Riley alongside articles by its usual reviewers Kerr and Barnes, and it published an article by Thomas Johnson titled 'The Black Theatergoer: Who Is He?' (1970), which reflected on the demographics of New York's theatre scene and the dominant whiteness of the theatre establishment. *Slave Ship* would also go on tour in the South the following year in a production by the Free Southern Theater also directed by Moses. There, it was performed before almost exclusively black audiences in churches, schools, and other community spaces. In this context, where spectators were largely 'working people, farmers, and share-croppers with an awareness of their subservient position within a system of economic and cultural oppression' (Elam, 1996, p. 26), the revolutionary spirit at the end of the performance was reportedly heightened (Elam, p. 13). One practical effect of this tour, noted by Moses, was increased participation in voter registration drives in the cities where the piece played (Elam, p. 13).

Difficult discussions

Both *Votes for Women!* and *Slave Ship* involved their audiences in acts of political protest by introducing theatrical techniques that blurred the boundaries between the world of the play and the world of political action beyond the play. In other words, as audience members became participants in the fictional realms of the plays, they simultaneously participated in actions that had genuine political relevance. For the uninitiated, such experiences had the potential to be a galvanizing force that could lead to action outside of the theatre as well. Importantly, both plays were able to achieve these effects because they were performed in relation to very specific and recognizable political movements with which those who wrote, directed, and acted in the plays were personally involved. They did not spark protests out of the blue, but served as one among many strategies for activating audiences around vital concerns of the day.

Achieving this confluence between a successful piece of theatre and a political movement is not easy, however. As political movements themselves and the problems they seek to address change, successful techniques of the past also require continual revision. To consider some of the challenges of engaging audiences in an act of protest in the theatre, I turn to a more recent production, created in response to the international Occupy movement: a new interpretation of Ibsen's *Enemy of the People* ([1882], 2012) by Berlin's Schaubühne theatre company, directed by Thomas Ostermeier.

Ibsen's play follows the story of Dr Thomas Stockman, who discovers that the baths in his town, which are its main source of revenue, are contaminated with toxins from a factory upstream. Stockman undertakes to reveal this information to the townspeople, and at first he has a number of supporters, including the editors of the local newspaper, who will publish his findings. However, the mayor of the town, who happens to be Stockman's brother, convinces Stockman's friends at the paper that repairing the baths would be financially disastrous for the town, so they withdraw their offer to publish Stockman's article. Stockman then decides to call a town meeting where he will reveal that the baths are polluted. Yet again, the mayor intervenes and encourages the town to vote against allowing Stockman to speak. In response, Stockman launches into a scathing critique of what he refers to as the 'compact Liberal majority' – the majority whose opinions are led by the few – which he describes as 'the most dangerous enemy of truth and freedom'. The town reacts by declaring him an enemy of the people. At the end of the play, Stockman remains true to his own moral compass but he and his family are ruined: he and his daughter, as well as a family friend, are fired from their jobs, his family are evicted from their home, and they are cut out of his father-in-law's will.

The play is in keeping with what Shaw called a discussion play: it presents difficult problems that are not resolved by the play but that the audience is meant to consider and talk over. These problems include questions about the functioning of majority rule; the place of free thinking within liberal democracies; the sometimes competing responsibilities of individuals towards their families, their communities, and their principles; and the role of the economy within a liberal democracy, particularly when conflicts of interest exist between maintaining the economy and taking care of people's health and the environment. Though originally written well over 100 years ago, such questions are certainly still relevant today and worth discussing.

For Ostermeier, the play's critique of the economy, and its exploration of 'how political movements or certain ecological truths are suppressed by economic interests', spoke directly to the defeat of the Occupy movement, which he claims inspired him to direct *Enemy of the People* (Nickl and Schellenberg, 2014). Basing his production on an adaptation by company dramaturg Florian Borchmeyer, Ostermeier stylishly updated the setting to the contemporary moment, casting the characters as young, urban hipsters. At the same time, Ostermeier aimed to go beyond the format of the discussion play, where the conversation among audience members happens after the curtain call, and sought to activate such a conversation during the show. He did so, similarly to *Votes for Women!*, by incorporating the audience into the town hall meeting of Act IV and inviting audience members to join in a political discussion.

The scene was widely celebrated by critics. Reviewing the production at the Barbican Theatre in 2014, which I attended, *Guardian* critic Michael Billington went so far as to declare, 'I've rarely seen a more exciting use of audience participation than in Thomas Ostermeier's Berlin Schaubühne production of Ibsen's play.' For him, the 'tactic release[d] a genuine anger against consensual politics, with various people shouting "stop bonuses" and "pay more taxes"'. Billington suggests that the scene brought contentious politics into the theatre and this in itself was a big part of its exhilaration. Yet, in my experience, there were also limitations to the gesture, which stemmed from a persistent incongruence between the world of the play and the action in the auditorium.

Key to Borchmeyer's adaptation is an attempt to link Ibsen's text directly to contemporary discourse. The most striking move in this direction occurs during Stockman's speech. After announcing that he will not speak about the baths at all, but about something of much greater significance, namely the poisoning of all of civic society, Stockman declares that the greatest problem of the contemporary moment is 'mass personalization'. The phrase comes from a 2007 French anarchist manifesto titled *The Coming Insurrection*, written by an anonymous group called The Invisible Committee. From this point on, Stockman's speech is largely drawn from this text, which has been closely associated with the Occupy movement. The speech is a wide-ranging meditation on the ills of contemporary society. It speaks about the feelings of emptiness that come from trying to claim a sense of identity in a context in which maximizing the perceived value of the self (through the achievement of certain lifestyle aims, for example) has become an imperative at the expense of relations between people: 'The more I want to be me, the more I feel the emptiness. […] I manage, you manage, we manage our "I" like a money-counter in a bank,' Stockman intones, echoing *The Coming Insurrection*. He decries the falseness of the contemporary 'I', which is 'sharply defined and separate', but only in order to be made 'assessable, classable', and, ultimately, 'controllable', and he despairs of the contemporary family, which only serves to mask the deepening separations between people. At the root of these problems lies the economy, which the text declares is not 'in' crisis, as is usually said, but *is* the crisis insofar as economic interests control all other interests. At the same time, the speech questions the approaches of a certain liberal class to this crisis – approaches that implore people to 'become joyously frugal. Eat organic, ride your bike', and embrace 'voluntary simplicity' – arguing that such attempts to respond to the crisis only contribute to its perpetuation. It is, in sum, a complex and challenging speech. It is a text that demands discussion.

Yet, the night I attended, the audience did not discuss Stockman's speech or rally around the issues that it raises. When Stockman's brother turned to the audience, asking if we agreed with Stockman, most hands in the auditorium went up, indicating a widespread dissatisfaction with the current economic situation. However, rather than probing the issues raised by the speech (issues that are more complex than one sweeping gesture of agreement would imply), what followed was an open invitation to the audience to discuss whatever we felt was of vital importance. Two things happened: On the one hand, several people raised contemporary concerns. One person commented on the impending Scottish independence referendum, for example. But the German actors, tasked with responding and facilitating the discussion, had difficulty directing the suggested topics towards a coherent conversation. Thus, various people expressed opinions on disparate concerns, but no single subject took off. On the other hand, several people seemed to ignore the fact that Stockman's speech had moved us far away from the matter of the baths, and, feeling themselves cast as members of the town hall meeting, expressed opinions about the state of affairs within the world of the play, for instance by passing judgement on the characters or suggesting what they ought to do. These two approaches remained strangely at odds with one another.

Whereas *Votes for Women!* and *Slave Ship* incorporated their audiences in ways that allowed them *both* to become part of the play *and* to participate in political action in the theatre, there was in (my experience of) *Enemy of the People* an odd disjuncture between, rather than a joining together of, the world of the play and the real world issues that the audience was attempting to engage.

Part of the difficulty facing audience members trying to find their feet in this scene is that the Schaubühne's *Enemy of the People* encourages the audience to act *against* the direction of the play. In other words, it seems to place the audience in the position of the townspeople, who in the play denounce Stockman, while expecting that they will largely agree with him instead. Thus, for *New York Times* reviewer Charles Isherwood, who disliked the audience participation ('Most of us prefer to express [our political views] at the polls, not the theater,' he asserted), 'the audience was playing precisely the wrong role' (2013). Given this tension, the only way for a Stockman-supporting audience's contributions to feel truly meaningful would be for them to be capable of altering the course of the play, or ending it. Interestingly, in video footage of the production in Moscow, where the audience appears to have become intensely engaged to the point of coming up on stage, the actor playing Stockman, Christoph Gawenda, is shown eventually asking the audience if they still want to see Scene V. The audience laughs and claps in the affirmative (Nickl and Schellenberg). Yet, to return to the play at this point with its pre-scripted ending is also to turn away from the audience's readiness to engage in

some form of political action. Furthermore, instead of concluding with a sense of potential, the play ends by questioning whether anyone, including Stockman and, by extension,
the audience, can truly act beyond economic interests: when
Stockman's father-in-law hands him shares in the polluting
factory, Stockman does not destroy them as Ibsen's hero
does, but is left staring at them with his wife, their decision uncertain as the lights go down. It is a provocative ending, certainly, which refuses to romanticize the image of the
steadfast activist, committed to his cause against all odds,
but it also defeats the politicized energy that the play worked
to generate among audience members just moments earlier.

Perhaps the biggest contradiction during the London run
is that at the same time that *Enemy of the People* was promis-
ing and failing to turn the Barbican Theatre into a place
for political action, *Exhibit B* was being withdrawn by the
Barbican from the Waterloo Vaults across town. As my col-
league Alan Read suggested at the time, maybe we should
have been discussing that.

Re-actions

I have been focusing on theatre-in-theatres as a particular
point of tension between theatre and protest. I have recon-
sidered a logic that would suggest that theatre needs to be
shielded from protest in order to protect its freedom of
expression and argued instead that protests against theatre
could be a contribution to it. I have also questioned assumptions that protests staged as part of plays are unable to
affect the world beyond them and that any overt attempt

to act politically in the theatre reduces it to mere 'propaganda'. In contrast, I have explored situations in which such attempts have made for both good politics and good theatre, while also pointing out some of the difficulties of achieving this synthesis. In this section, I explore some remaining tensions between theatre and protest, which extend beyond the space of the theatre *per se*. These emerge at a point where theatre has been overtly inspired by political action: in the re-enactment of historical protests by performers, sometimes in theatre and performance spaces and sometimes at the site of the original protests. Here, protest has not been perceived as a threat to (good) theatre so much as theatre has appeared to some to be a threat to protest, sapping it of its legitimacy and vitality. What happens when protest actions are re-enacted at some distance, temporally and/or geographically, from the original actions? What might this achieve?

Striking re-enactments

Once again, instances of theatrical re-enactments of protests can be found across the period we have been considering. An early example is the Paterson Strike Pageant (1913). The performance was conceived by Industrial Workers of the World (IWW) leader Bill Haywood, New York journalist John Reed (who served as director), and arts patron Mabel Dodge Luhan as a contribution to the IWW-led silk workers' strike in Paterson, New Jersey. Taking place during the ongoing strike, which had begun nearly four months earlier, the pageant aimed to recreate the events of the strike for New York audiences in an effort to raise awareness and support for the cause, as well as desperately needed funds for striking workers who were struggling to continue without wages. It was performed on 7 June 1913 in New York's Madison Square Garden – the largest performance hall in the world at that time – before an audience of over 15,000 people. Against a 200-foot backdrop portraying the Paterson silk mills, over 1,000 strikers along with major strike leaders (including Haywood and labour activist and feminist Elizabeth Gurley Flynn) performed as themselves in the pageant.

Across a series of 'episodes', the pageant re-enacted major scenes from the strike, which had taken place in the preceding months. It began on the first day, with workers leaving their looms and joining in the singing of 'La Marseillaise', the revolutionary French anthem; proceeded to show attacks on peaceful picketers by police and detectives hired by the manufacturers, which resulted in the fatal shooting of bystander Valentino Modestino on 17 April; portrayed the mournful funeral procession for Modestino; then drew spectators into a mass meeting, with rousing speeches from IWW leaders delivered to the performing strikers and the audience alike. A re-enactment of the May Day parade and a tearful scene of sending the striking workers' children to live with families in other cities comprised the fifth episode. The pageant concluded with further speeches, with the strikers affirming their commitment to the eight-hour workday for which they were fighting, and, finally, with the workers and the audience singing the 'Internationale', a standard of the socialist movement.

As a fundraiser, the pageant was a disappointment; it was expensive to produce and the highest priced seats had to be discounted at the last minute while several thousand tickets were given away to strikers, some of whom had walked the twenty-three miles from Paterson to see it. However, it was a success in generating support for the strike in New York. The New York *World* reported that 'few witnessed the exhibition without sympathy' (*World* review, quoted in *Current Opinion Magazine*, reprinted in Kornbluh, 2011, p. 212). Furthermore, it was widely praised for creating a mass spectacle unlike anything that had been seen before. It would also be credited with inspiring the perhaps more well-known *Storming of the Winter Palace* (1920), directed by Nikolai Evreinov, which re-enacted on its third anniversary the events of the Bolshevik 'October Revolution' on location in Petrograd (Dawson, 1999, p. 66).

For reviewers at the time, what made the Paterson strike re-enactment so moving was that it created an embodied encounter with the strike that felt emphatically *real*. The *Tribune* commented that whereas 'lesser geniuses might have hired a hall and exhibited moving pictures', the Paterson Pageant instead 'transported the strike itself bodily to New York' (*Tribune* review, quoted in *Current Opinion Magazine*, reprinted in Kornbluh, p. 212). Not only was the Paterson Pageant a live performance, which enabled audience members to feel part of the action as they listened to strike speeches and joined in the singing of strike songs, but the performers were actual strikers from Paterson. This lent an air of authenticity to the event and a feeling for viewers that

they were encountering the true personalities of the protestors. The *Survey*, for instance, asserted that '[t]he thing
that struck the observer most forcibly was the sort of people
the strikers seemed to be and the absence of race prejudice'
amongst the ethnically diverse workers. It referred to the
strikers performing as themselves as a 'human document'
and affirmed that the pageant 'gave a real acquaintance with
the spirit, point of view and earnestness of those who live
what a "human document" tells; it conveyed what speech
and pamphlet, picture and cartoon, fiction and drama fall
short of telling' (*Survey* review, reprinted in McNamara,
1971, p. 66).

Importantly, one of the things that appears to have been
most well regarded about the Paterson Strike Pageant is that
it was 'not a drama', as the *World* reported. The *Tribune* also
stressed that 'the pageant was without staginess or apparent
striving for theatrical effect'. And, the *International Socialist
Review* raved that 'Stage managers annually spend months of
toil on a "mob scene" that the Paterson strikers outclassed
with a single rehearsal. As a spectacle, it was perfect. Nowhere
was there a suggestion of "acting".' Instead, the performers
'simply lived their battles over again' (*International Socialist
Review* article, reprinted in McNamara, p. 67).

What emerges in the reviews of the Paterson Pageant
are both some of the perceived strengths and some of the
perceived risks of re-enactment in its bringing together of
theatre and political action. On the one hand, reviewers
celebrated the potential of re-enactment to transport a
protest action beyond the bounds of space and time in ways

that other media seemed unable to do. Creating an embodied encounter with the struggle – even a sense of participation in it, as strikers on stage and strikers in the audience along with New York audience members all sang together – the Paterson Pageant produced a sense of urgency that many felt exceeded the potential of other art forms. Yet, on the other hand, we also encounter one of the primary resistances to re-enactment, which emerges precisely at those points where re-enactment overlaps with theatre. The Paterson Pageant was praised specifically for *not* being a 'drama', for *avoiding* 'staginess', and for *abolishing* 'acting'. Clearly, the pageant *did* involve theatrical elements: the strikers performed *as if* they were in Paterson even though they were not; and they mourned over a coffin that did not, it is safe to assume, contain the body of Modestino. Yet, the pageant achieved the effect for which it was commended of *not* being theatre because the performers were actually strikers and not trained actors; because they portrayed events from the recent past that they themselves had lived through; and because the events they re-enacted were part of an ongoing struggle of which the pageant was also a part. All of these things made the pageant feel vital and real. However, we might also wonder why theatre should be perceived as such a detraction from re-enactment – something whose absence should be praised. We might also ask if it is possible for re-enactment to ever be fully divorced from theatre? What happens as re-enactment moves further away in time from the original event? Can it maintain the sense of urgency that the Paterson Pageant achieved?

Resounding calls to action

By way of contrast, let us consider a more recent set of protest
re-enactments: Mark Tribe's *Port Huron Project* (2006–2008).
Named for the 1962 manifesto of Students for a Democratic
Society, and described as 'a series of reenactments of protest speeches from the New Left movements of the Vietnam
era' (Tribe), the *Port Huron Project* included re-enactments of
speeches by: Coretta Scott King at a 1968 antiwar protest
in New York's Central Park; Howard Zinn at a 1971 peace
rally on Boston Common; Paul Potter at a 1965 March on
Washington against the Vietnam War; César Chávez at a
1971 Vietnam veterans memorial rally in Los Angeles's
Exposition Park; Angela Davis at a 1969 Black Panther rally
in DeFremery Park in Oakland, California; and Stokely
Carmichael at a 1967 antiwar protest outside the United
Nations in New York. Each speech was delivered by a hired
actor at the site of the original action before a live audience of invited spectators, recording crew, and passersby.
Videos of the re-enactments were subsequently screened in
art galleries and in public spaces such as Times Square in
New York, as well as being uploaded onto free-access sites
including YouTube.

Interestingly, though the performers were actors deliv-
ering speeches that had been written by others 40 years
before, Tribe was, like those who praised the Paterson
Pageant, keen to avoid any suggestion of theatricality. In his
statement on the project, Tribe asserts that 'the performers
did not attempt to look or sound like the original speakers;
I directed them to wear their everyday clothes and to

deliver the speeches in their own voices. I made no attempt to theatricalize the performances or to create any illusion of returning to the past.' His goal was to simply recreate the speeches without 'aesthetic adornments'. Yet, despite these statements, Tribe cast actors who resembled the original speakers in terms of gender, race, ethnicity, and age – a practice in line with the conventions of realist theatre and designed to enable the suspension of disbelief needed to view the person on stage *as if* they were the person they played (a practice, too, that demands careful consideration as it can make diversity visible but can also naturalize differences between people). Furthermore, at least some of the performers appear to have dressed for the part: For instance Gina Brown, who performed the speech by Coretta Scott King, wore a conservative blue skirt suit with a matching hat and pearls around her neck. The look clearly harkened to the past, and its formality set Brown apart as a performer from the spectators clad in jeans and T-shirts. Finally, all of the performers delivered the speeches with emotional intensity and actorly skill, conjuring the absent audiences from the 1960s whom they addressed, even as the present audiences stood in their place. Despite Tribe's stated aims, theatre and theatricality are surely in evidence in the *Port Huron Project*.

As a visual artist, it is possible that Tribe hoped to avoid a taint of theatricality that has often been perceived as a threat to good art, insofar as 'good art' is defined by its originality. As performance studies scholar Rebecca Schneider points out, re-enactments that bear the marks of theatre can also feel like downright bad art. For surely, most would say: the speech was great *the first time*! The second time is farce, fake, theatre. The first time was on target. The second time is way off, late, minor, drag, DIY, any-clown-can-do-it. The first time was true. The second time is false, etiolated, hollow, or infelicitous. The second time, the third time, the nth times are *not actual*. (2011, p. 180, Schneider's italics)

Here, we see how theatre, with all of its 'as ifs' (*as if* Brown were King; *as if* it were 1968), comes to be deplored as a false copy (for Brown is *not* King, and it is *not* 1968) and the opposite of the *real*. For the visual arts, which have long placed value in originals, this sense of being a mere copy has also meant that theatricality has often been viewed as a negation of good art. Yet, we might also suggest that theatre, *as an art*, is essential to the *Port Huron Project* precisely insofar as theatre is a medium of re-enacting, which is to say, it is an art that is realized in the re-saying of words and the re-doing of actions by multiple people across space and time.

At the same time, there are those for whom such questions about 'good art' versus 'bad art' are beside the point. For them, the problem with (theatrical) re-enactment lies in its aim to be art at all. Thus, for media studies scholar Paige Sarlin, the problem with the *Port Huron Project* is that it is '*not a political project*' (2009, p. 142, emphasis added). Rather, she argues, its 'sense of vision and direction are tied entirely to the realm of cultural production', and thus it is an example of how 'a political project is transformed into an aesthetic or cultural practice' (p. 143). In other words, to the extent that the *Port Huron Project* circulates primarily within the realm of art, both in terms of who was involved in making it and which audiences it aims to reach (both points on which it differs from the Paterson Pageant), it could seem to reproduce the past as an aesthetic object without engaging in any active politics.

Thus, a familiar set of tensions between 'good art' and 'bad art', 'good politics' and 'bad politics' arises when theatre and protest come together in re-enactment. Yet, once again I want to argue that the re-enactment of protest can make good art *and* have political effects.

Tribe, who was teaching at Brown University in Rhode Island at the time of the *Port Huron Project*, claims to have been motivated by his students' lack of political activism. Though many of them were opposed to the then ongoing Iraq War, they seemed to be convinced, Tribe found, of the uselessness of protesting against it. They were not alone. Indeed, a repeated sentiment in the first decade of the twenty-first century was that protest no longer worked. The failure of the largest protest event in history, the anti-war protest of 15 February 2003 in which up to 30 million people around the globe participated, to prevent the invasion of Iraq was seen by many as a sign that protest could no longer effect change. In response, the *Port Huron Project* aimed to bring to life the words and ideas of a generation who believed that they could end the war and change the world (and who many would say achieved their aims). At a basic level, then, the project had pedagogical aims to teach a younger generation (and remind an older generation) about the discourses and practices of dissent that had animated the 1960s. It also had more overtly political aspirations to inspire this generation to act themselves.

One can learn a lot from watching the videos of the speeches selected for the project. Together, they make a persuasive case for the interrelatedness of various concerns, as one after another leaders of the civil rights, Black Power, student, United Farm Workers, and antiwar movements draw connections between US militarism abroad and its treatment of labourers, poor people, and racial minorities at home. More strikingly, the connections to the present (*both* to the time of the project's creation *and* to the moment nearly 10 years later when I am writing) resound again and again. When Max Bunzel, speaking Paul Potter's words, says that the current war has 'led to even more vigorous governmental efforts to control information, manipulate the press and pressure and persuade the public through distorted and downright dishonest documents', audience members in 2007 are likely to have thought about the forged intelligence documents that US and British governments used in 2002 to confirm that Iraq was developing weapons of mass destruction. (The documents were revealed to be fake in 2003.) When Matthew Floyd Miller, speaking Howard Zinn's words, proclaims that it is 'time to impeach [the] President [...] who carries on this war', audiences in 2007 may well have thought of ongoing calls to impeach then President George W. Bush for illegally waging war in Iraq. (That effort culminated in 2008 with the US House of Representatives voting in favour of referring a 35-point impeachment resolution to the Judiciary Committee, where the resolution remained as Bush's presidency ended soon after.) Watching the speeches today, at a time when repeated instances in the US of police killing unarmed black men have led many to call police violence a form of domestic terrorism, I am struck by Angela Davis's words (delivered by Sheilagh Brooks) that 'terror is becoming not just isolated instances of police brutality here and there, but [...] an everyday instrument of the institutions of this country'.

Of course, such echoes are not without their ambivalence. As Tribe himself notes, seeing how relevant the New Left's critiques remain today could also lead one to the despairing conclusion that 'the revolutionary solutions the New Left imagined are beyond us' (Tribe). Rather than being inspired, one might be left with the feeling that their promise was not fulfilled. Furthermore, those watching the speeches live as part of small gatherings, more in line with the size of performance art audiences than with the thousands present at the historical protests, and those watching the videos online, perhaps alone at home, might feel conscious of their very distance from any real political action.

Yet, the *Port Huron Project* also stages and makes palpable the embodied passion and commitment required for any political act. One after another, the speakers do their best to rally the people, to impart a demand for action from which they will not be able to turn away. Writing about the *Port*

Huron Project, Schneider asks, 'When does a call to action, cast into the future, fully take place? Only in the moment of the call? Or can a call to action be resonant in the varied and reverberant cross-temporal spaces where an echo might encounter response – even years and years later?' (2011, p. 181). Certainly, it is impossible not to feel directly spoken to when Max Bunzel as Paul Potter calls for 'people who are willing to change their lives, who are willing to challenge the system, to take the problem of change seriously'; when Ricardo Dominguez as César Chávez says, 'Nothing less than organized, disciplined nonviolent action that goes on every day will challenge the power of the corporations and the generals. The problem is that people have to decide to do it'; or when Ato Essandoh as Stokely Carmichael says, 'It is up to you!'

Finally, perhaps protest re-enactment also answers to a need to hear such messages more than once. Something not visible in the videos of the *Port Huron Project* is that at least some of the live performances were repeated several times to get the desired camera angles. Writing about the re-enactment of Chávez's speech in 2008, *Los Angeles Times* art critic Christopher Knight reported that at the end of the *second* iteration, the audience spontaneously erupted into a chant of 'Si, se puede!' (Spanish for 'Yes, it can be done!'), the United Farm Workers (UFW) slogan that Chávez and co-founder Dolores Huerta coined in 1972, which has been adopted by many political movements since. Chávez's speech did not include these words, but the slogan was being used at the time by Barack Obama in his 'Yes we can!' campaign

(Obama acknowledged that he had taken the phrase from the UFW and used the Spanish version on several occasions). As the spectators chanted, they might have been responding to Chávez's words *and* they might have been rallying in support of Obama. Clearly, the resonance was there, but it took the audience hearing the speech twice to fully connect past and present and to give voice to a call for a better future.

A gesture towards an end

If the *Port Huron Project* was made at a time of despair about the possibility of protest, the years since have seen a dramatic rise in protest activity. From the breathtaking protests of the 'Arab Spring', which began in Tunisia in 2010, to the global Occupy movement, which began in New York in 2011, to the international Black Lives Matter movement, which emerged as the hashtag #BlackLivesMatter in 2013, to name just a few, protest movements seem once again to be a major social and political force. So striking was the sense that protest had *returned* as a viable activity in the second decade of the twenty-first century that *Time* magazine named 'the protester' its 'Person of the Year' in December 2011. In the cover story, Kurt Anderson asserts that for the previous two decades, since 1991,

> street protests looked like pointless emotional sideshows — obsolete, quaint, the equivalent of cavalry to mid-20th-century war. The rare large demonstrations in the rich world seemed ineffectual and irrelevant. (See the Battle of Seattle [in response

> to a meeting of the World Trade Organization], 1999.) [...] 'Massive and effective street protest' was a global oxymoron until — suddenly, shockingly — starting exactly a year ago, it became the defining trope of our times.

That Anderson doesn't even mention the antiwar protest of 15 February 2003 seems only to confirm how overlooked that event was *and* how drastically things appeared to have changed by the end of 2011.

Much could be said about this new wave of protest movements. For instance, their use of social media to spread news, to raise awareness, and to organize actions has marked a profound shift in how protest operates. But there is another remarkable feature that has emerged in recent years, more directly relevant to the discussion here, and this is the conspicuous use (and reuse) of theatrical gestures both to convey protest messages and to spread these messages across bodies.

Some of the most powerful of these gestures have been made as protests against state-sanctioned violence against black people in the United States. In 2013, when George Zimmerman was acquitted for fatally shooting 17-year-old Trayvon Martin in a Florida suburb, protestors declared 'I am Trayvon', often while wearing hoodies and carrying packs of Skittles candy, as Martin had been when he was shot. In 2014, after Eric Garner was killed by a police officer who placed him in an illegal chokehold and ignored Garner (who was asthmatic) repeatedly stating 'I can't breathe', another gesture emerged as protestors repeated Garner's words, sometimes written on tape across their mouths. Less than one month later, when Michael Brown, an unarmed black teenager, was shot 12 times by a white police officer while reportedly holding his hands up in surrender, perhaps the most emblematic and lasting gesture of the movement was born as protestors raised their hands in the air with the words 'Hands up, don't shoot!'

Such gestures differ from other protest slogans and signs, such as 'No justice, no peace!' or the Black Power salute, in their particular theatricality. For, to say 'I am Trayvon' is a theatrical gesture, not because the protestors pretend to be Martin or try to give the illusion that they are him, but because they stand in for him in his absence, and in doing so show that all black bodies are at risk within structures of systemic racism. When white activists began supporting the movement by posting pictures of themselves on social media with the words 'I am not Trayvon Martin', followed by a statement condemning the system that allowed him to be killed – a gesture meant to acknowledge that the killing of Martin was a specifically racist act and that not all bodies are treated the same – they engaged with important questions of theatre: who can stand in for whom, and how do different bodies signify differently? When protestors chant or wear T-shirts saying 'I can't breathe', or seal their mouths with those words, they also seek to embody Eric Garner in his final moments, to make his death felt again through the replaying of his words. In doing so, they also enable Garner's last words to resound as a broader

statement about the stifling experience of living in a state that tolerates police brutality. And when protestors raise their hands in a gesture of surrender, they perform their solidarity with Michael Brown and show themselves to be like him, vulnerable. It is a gesture that says 'I am within your power', and thus its repeated re-enactment – including at moments when those performing it might not appear to be at risk, such as when NFL football players, or members of the US House of Representatives, or the cast members of the film *Selma* have performed the gesture – becomes a demand on power to do what is right.

Those who perform these gestures seem to know, implicitly at least, something that the theatre knows: the affective and instructive power of embodying the speech and actions of others; the importance of witnessing and responding to such acts; and the value of repeating them, again.

further reading

As should be clear, there are many ways to approach the question of the relationship between theatre and protest. My aim here has been to track and analyze specific points of intersection and tension between these forms across the twentieth and twenty-first centuries. My aim has not been (nor would it have been possible) to provide a comprehensive overview of all of the literature related to activist performance and/or the performance of protest. For those wishing to embark on further research, the following are some suggestions, grouped around different approaches you might take. These divisions are not discrete, and some of the texts could be grouped differently. This list is also not exhaustive, but these texts provide a valuable starting point.

For those wanting to find out more about **grassroots activist theatre**, the companies that developed in the 1960s have by far received the most attention. See: Harry Elam, *Taking It to the Streets*; James Harding and Cindy

Rosenthal, eds. *Restaging the Sixties*; Claudia Orenstein, *Festive Revolutions*; and Eugène van Erven, *Radical People's Theatre*. A number of these companies are also still making work, so check out their websites and go to see them if you can. For earlier periods, Sheila Stowell's *A Stage of Their Own* and Raphael Samuel, Ewan MacColl, and Stuart Cosgrove's *Theatres of the Left* are excellent resources on suffragette theatre and the Worker's Theatre Movement, respectively.

A number of books on **creative activism and art (as) activism** have been published in recent years. Some of these offer a 'how to' approach while others focus more on documenting, describing, and analyzing such actions. See: L.M. Bogad, *Tactical Performance* and *Electoral Guerrilla Theatre*; Andrew Boyd and Dave Oswald Mitchell, eds. *Beautiful Trouble*; Angelique Haugerud, *No Billionaire Left Behind*; steirischer herbst and Florian Malzacher, eds. *Truth Is Concrete*; Robert Klanten et al., eds. *Art & Agenda*; Nato Thompson and Gregory Sholette, eds. *Interventionists*; and Nato Thompson, ed. *Living as Form.*

The field of performance studies has been defined by its broad approach to performance, and protest has been an important part of this expanded field. For **performance studies approaches to protest**, often thought alongside theatre and other performance forms (and often wrestling with the tensions between them that I have explored here), see: Jan Cohen-Cruz, ed. *Radical Street Performance*; Jenny Edkins and Adrian Kear, eds. *International Politics and Performance*; Baz Kershaw, *The Radical in Performance*; Peter Lichtenfels and John Rouse, eds. *Performance, Politics and Activism*; D. Soyini

Madison, *Acts of Activism*; Bradford D. Martin, *The Theater Is in the Street*; Shirin M. Rai and Janelle Reinelt, eds. *The Grammar of Politics and Performance*; David Román, *Acts of Intervention*; Benjamin Shepard, *Play, Creativity, and Social Movements*; Jenny Spencer, ed. *Political and Protest Theatre After 9/11*; and Diana Taylor, *The Archive and the Repertoire*. I have been focusing on books, but Susan Leigh Foster's article 'Choreographies of Protest' also deserves mention as an influential contribution from dance studies. Finally, the following special journal issues also provide a useful map of how ideas about theatre and activism have developed over the twenty-first century: *Theater and Social Change*, Special Issue of *Theater*, ed. Alisa Solomon (2001); *Theatre and Activism*, Special Issue of *Theatre Journal*, ed. Harry Elam (2003), and *Theatre, Performance and Activism: Gestures towards an Equitable World*, Special Issue of *Contemporary Theatre Review*, eds. Jenny Hughes and Simon Parry (2015).

references

Andersen, Kurt. 'Person of the Year 2011: The Protester.' *Time*. 14 December 2011. http://content.time.com/time/specials/packages/article/0,28804,2101745_2102132,00.html?xid=newsletter-daily [accessed 6 April 2017].

Anderson, Sharon J. 'Interview with Playwright Barbara Hammond.' 2015. http://catf.org/we-are-pussy-riot-by-barbara-hammond/ [accessed 6 April 2017].

Bailey, Brett. 'Yes, Exhibit B Is Challenging – But I Never Sought to Alienate or Offend.' *Guardian*. Opinion. 24 September 2014. https://www.theguardian.com/commentisfree/2014/sep/24/exhibit-b-challenging-work-never-sought-alienate-offend-brett-bailey [accessed 6 April 2017].

Balme, Christopher. *The Theatrical Public Sphere*. Cambridge, UK: Cambridge University Press, 2014.

Barbican. 'Statement on the Cancellation of *Exhibit B*.' https://www.barbican.org.uk/news/artformnews/theatredance/barbican-statement-cancellation- [accessed 6 April 2017].

Barnes, Clive. 'The Theater: New LeRoi Jones Play: "Slave Ship" Presented by Chelsea Center.' *New York Times*. 22 November 1969. Proquest Historical Newspapers: The New York Times. 46.

Benford, Robert D. and Scott A. Hunt. 'Dramaturgy and Social Movements: The Social Construction and Communication of Power.' *Sociological Inquiry* 62.1 (1992): 36–55.

Billington, Michael. 'An Enemy of the People Five-Star Review – Like a Rowdy Version of Question Time.' *Guardian*. Theatre. 25 September 2014. https://www.theguardian.com/stage/2014/sep/25/an-enemy-of-the-people-review-michael-billington [accessed 6 April 2017].

Blackadder, Neil. *Performing Opposition: Modern Theater and the Scandalized Audience*. Westport, CT: Praeger, 2003.

Boal, Augusto. *Theatre of the Oppressed*. Trans. Charles A. and Maria-Odilia Leal McBride. New York, NY: Theatre Communications Group, 1985 [1979].

Bogad, L.M. *Electoral Guerrilla Theatre: Radical Ridicule and Social Movements*. New York, NY: Routledge, 2005.

Bogad, L.M. *Tactical Performance: The Theory and Practice of Serious Play*. Abingdon, UK: Routledge, 2016.

Boyd, Andrew and Dave Oswald Mitchell, eds. *Beautiful Trouble: A Toolbox for Revolution*. New York, NY: OR Books, 2012.

Brecht, Bertolt. *Brecht on Theatre: The Development of an Aesthetic*. Trans. John Willett. New York, NY: Hill and Wang, 1964.

Brustein, Robert. *The Theatre of Revolt: An Approach to the Modern Drama*. Boston, MA: Little Brown, 1964.

Cohen-Cruz, Jan, ed. *Radical Street Performance: An International Anthology*. London, UK: Routledge, 1998.

Contemporary American Theatre Festival. 'Email Advertisement for *We Are Pussy Riot*.' 2015. http://us4.campaign-archive2.com/?u=20436d12392819be5a2b4cae2&id=a605187133&e=f957ba0204 [accessed 6 April 2017].

Davis, R.G. *The San Francisco Mime Troupe: The First Ten Years*. Palo Alto, CA: Ramparts, 1975.

Dawson, Gary Fischer. *Documentary Theatre in the United States: An Historical Survey and Analysis of Its Content, Form and Stagecraft.* Westport, CT: Greenwood Publishing Group, 1999.

D'Urso, Sandra. 'On the Theology of Romeo Castellucci's Theatre and the Politics of the Christian "Occupation" of His Stage.' *Theatre Research International* 38.1 (2013): 34–46.

Edkins, Jenny and Adrian Kear, eds. *International Politics and Performance: Critical Aesthetics and Creative Practice.* Abingdon, UK: Routledge, 2013.

Elam, Harry. 'Social Urgency, Audience Participation, and the Performance of *Slave Ship* by Amiri Baraka.' *Crucibles of Crisis: Performing Social Change.* Ed. Janelle Reinelt. Ann Arbor, MI: University of Michigan Press, 1996. 13–35.

Elam, Harry. *Taking It to the Streets: The Social Protest Theater of Luis Valdez and Amiri Baraka.* Ann Arbor, MI: University of Michigan Press, 1997.

Elam, Harry, ed. *Theatre and Activism,* Special Issue of *Theatre Journal* 55.4 (December 2003).

Ellis, Samantha. 'Votes for Women! Royal Court, April 1907.' *Guardian.* Theatre. 19 March 2003. https://www.theguardian.com stage/2003/mar/19/theatre.artsfeatures1 [accessed 6 April 2017].

el teatro campesino. 'Our History.' http://elteatrocampesino.com/ our-history/ [accessed 6 April 2017].

Foster, Susan Leigh. 'Choreographies of Protest.' *Theatre Journal* 55.3 (2003): 395–412.

Gessen, Masha. 'A Pale Reflection of Reality.' *New York Times.* Opinion. 4 March 2013. http://latitude.blogs.nytimes.com/2013/03/04/ in-russia-political-theater-becomes-life-in-the-moscow-trials/ [accessed 6 April 2017].

Gottfried, Martin. 'America's Most Exciting New Theatre?' *New York Times.* 21 February 1971. ProQuest Historical Newspapers: The New York Times. D3.

Handke, Peter. 'Theater-in-the-Street and Theater-in-Theaters' [1969]. *Radical Street Performance: An International Anthology.* Ed. Jan Cohen-Cruz. London: Routledge, 1998. 7–10.

Hankin, St. John. 'Realism at the Court.' *The Academy*. (13 April 1907). 369–370.

Harding, James and Cindy Rosenthal, eds. *Restaging the Sixties: Radical Theaters and Their Legacies*. Ann Arbor, MI: University of Michigan Press, 2006.

Haugerud, Angelique. *No Billionaire Left Behind: Satirical Activism in America*. Stanford, CA: Stanford University Press, 2013.

Hughes, Jenny and Simon Parry, eds. *Theatre, Performance and Activism: Gestures Towards an Equitable World*, Special Issue of *Contemporary Theatre Review* 25.3 (July 2015).

Invisible Committee. *The Coming Insurrection*. Los Angeles, CA: Semiotext(e), 2009. (Originally published as *L'insurrection qui vient* by Editions La Fabrique: Paris, 2007.)

Isherwood, Charles. 'An Ibsen Who Rages Over Ritalin and Economic Austerity Plans: A Contemporary "Enemy of the People" at the Harvey Theater.' *New York Times*. 7 November 2013. http://www.nytimes.com/2013/11/08/theater/reviews/a-contemporary-enemy-of-the-people-at-the-harvey-theater.html?_r=0 [accessed 6 April 2017].

Johnson, Thomas A. 'The Black Theatergoer: Who Is He?' *New York Times*. 21 January 1970. ProQuest Historical Newspapers: The New York Times. 35.

Kerr, Walter. 'Is This Their Dream? Is This Their New Dream?' *New York Times*. 23 November 1969. ProQuest Historical Newspapers: The New York Times. D1.

Kershaw, Baz. *The Radical in Performance: Between Brecht and Baudrillard*. London, UK: Routledge, 1999.

Klanten, Robert et al., eds. *Art & Agenda: Political Art and Activism*. Berlin: Gestalten, 2011.

Knight, Christopher. 'Mark Tribe's Port Huron Project via Los Angeles Contemporary Exhibitions.' *Los Angeles Times*. 25 July 2008. http://www.mutualart.com/OpenExternalArticle/Mark-Tribe-s-Port-Huron-Project-via-Los-/FAC3C751F6A56F0E [accessed 6 April 2017].

Kornbluh, Joyce L., ed. *Rebel Voices: An IWW Anthology*. Oakland, CA: PM Press, 2011.

Kushner, Tony, Holly Hughes et al. 'How Do You Make Social Change?' *Theater* 31.3 (2001): 62–93.

Lichtenfels, Peter and John Rouse, eds. *Performance, Politics and Activism*. Basingstoke, UK: Palgrave Macmillan, 2012.

Madison, D. Soyini. *Acts of Activism: Human Rights as Radical Performance*. Cambridge, UK: Cambridge University Press, 2010.

Martin, Bradford D. *The Theater Is in the Street: Politics and Performance in Sixties America*. Amherst, MA: University of Massachusetts Press, 2004.

McDonald, Jan. '"The Second Act Was Glorious": The Staging of the Trafalgar Scene from *Votes for Women!* at the Court Theatre.' *Theatre History Studies* 15 (June 1995): 139–160.

McGuinness, Caoimhe Mader. 'Protesting *Exhibit B* in London: Reconfiguring Antagonism as the Claiming of Theatrical Space.' *Contemporary Theatre Review* 26.2 (2016): 211–226.

McNamara, Brooks, ed. 'Paterson Strike Pageant.' *The Drama Review: TDR* 15.3 (Summer 1971): 60–71.

Myers, Sara. 'Withdraw the Racist Exhibition "Exhibit B – The Human Zoo" from Showing at the Barbican from 23rd–27th September.' Petition. 2014. https://www.change.org/p/withdraw-the-racist-exhibition-exhibition-b-the-human-zoo [accessed 6 April 2017].

Nickl, Andreas and Matthias Schellenberg, Directors. *'Ein Volksfiend' in Istanbul, London, und Moskau*. Film. Schaubühne. 2014.

Oliver, Robert Michael. 'Spine: Review of "We Are Pussy Riot" at Contemporary American Theater Festival.' *DC Metro Theater Arts*. 1 August 2015. http://dcmetrotheaterarts.com/2015/08/01/spine-review-of-we-are-pussy-riot-at-contemporary-american-theater-festival/ [accessed 6 April 2017].

O'Mahony, John. 'Edinburgh's Most Controversial Show: Exhibit B, A Human Zoo.' *Guardian*. 11 August 2014. https://www.theguardian.com/stage/2014/aug/11/-sp-exhibit-b-human-zoo-edinburgh-festivals-most-controversial [accessed 6 April 2017].

Orenstein, Claudia. *Festive Revolutions: The Politics of Popular Theater and the San Francisco Mime Troup*. Jackson, MS: University Mississippi Press, 1999.

Parsons, Michael. 'Hilary Mantel's Thatcher Tale, Exhibit B and the Failure to Tell Facts from Fantasy.' *Guardian*. Letter. 30 September 2014. https://www.theguardian.com/culture/2014/sep/30/hilary-mantel-thatcher-exhibit-b-facts-fantasy [accessed 6 April 2017].

Pinter, Harold. 'Nobel Lecture: Art, Truth, and Politics.' 2005. http://www.nobelprize.org/nobel_prizes/literature/laureates/2005/pinter-lecture-e.html [accessed 6 April 2017].

Rai, Shirin M. and Janelle Reinelt, eds. *The Grammar of Politics and Performance*. Abingdon, UK: Routledge, 2015.

Riley, Clayton. 'A Black View of "Slave Ship": Art Is What Moves You.' *New York Times.* 23 November, 1969. ProQuest Historical Newspapers: The New York Times. D3.

Román, David. *Acts of Intervention: Performance, Gay Culture, and AIDS*. Bloomington, IN: Indiana University Press, 1998.

Samuel, Raphael, Ewan MacColl, and Stuart Cosgrove. *Theatres of the Left: 1880–1935: Workers' Theatre Movements in Britain and America*. London, UK: Routledge & Kegan Paul, 1985.

Sarlin, Paige. 'New Left-Wing Melancholy: Mark Tribe's "The Port Huron Project" and the Politics of Reenactment.' *Framework: The Journal of Cinema and Media* 50.1/2 (Spring and Fall 2009): 139–157.

Schneider, Rebecca. *Performing Remains: Art and War in Times of Theatrical Reenactment*. Abingdon, UK: Routledge, 2011.

Sharp, Gene. *Sharp's Dictionary of Power and Struggle: Language of Civil Resistance in Conflicts*. New York, NY: Oxford University Press, 2012.

Shaw, George Bernard. *The Quintessence of Ibsenism: Now Completed to the Death of Ibsen*. New York, NY: Hill and Wang, 1958 [1913].

Shepard, Benjamin. *Play, Creativity, and Social Movements: If I Can't Dance, It's Not My Revolution*. New York, NY: Routledge, 2011.

Solomon, Alisa, ed. *Theater and Social Change*, Special Issue of *Theater* 31.3 (2001).

Spencer, Jenny, ed. *Political and Protest Theatre after 9/11: Patriotic Dissent*. New York, NY: Routledge, 2012.

steirischer herbst and Florian Malzacher, eds. *Truth Is Concrete: A Handbook for Artistic Strategies in Real Politics*. Berlin: Sternberg, 2014.

Stowell, Sheila. *A Stage of Their Own: Feminist Playwrights of the Suffrage Era*. Ann Arbor, MI: University of Michigan Press, 1994.

Taylor, Diana. *The Archive and the Repertoire: Performing Cultural Memory in the Americas*. Durham, NC: Duke University Press, 2003.

Third World Bunfight. 'Exhibit B.' http://thirdworldbunfight.co.za/
    exhibit-b/ [accessed 6 April 2017].

Thompson, Nato, ed. *Living as Form: Socially Engaged Art from 1991–2011*.
    New York, NY: Creative Time Books/Cambridge, MA: MIT Press,
    2012.

Thompson, Nato and Gregory Sholette, eds. *The Interventionists: Users'
    Manual for the Creative Disruption of Everyday Life*. North Adams, MA:
    MASS MoCA Publications/Cambridge, MA: MIT Press, 2004.

Tilly, Charles. *Contentious Performances*. Cambridge, UK: Cambridge
    University Press, 2008.

Tribe, Mark. 'The Port Huron Project.' https://www.marktribe.net/
    port-huron-project/ [accessed 6 April 2017].

Van Erven, Eugène. *Radical People's Theatre*. Bloomington, IN: Indiana
    University Press, 2000.

Wren, Celia. '2015 Contemporary American Theater Festival Sets the
    Stage for Rebellion.' *The Washington Post*. 15 July 2015. https://www.
    washingtonpost.com/entertainment/theater_dance/2015-
    contemporary-american-theater-festival-sets-the-stage-for-
    rebellion/2015/07/14/f539db08-2a4f-11e5-a250-42bd812efc09_
    story.html [accessed 6 April 2017].

index